Congratulations! However this book found you, you've taken the first step towards the beginning of a wonderful new adventure...now let it unfold...

Connect to Authentic Success: 7 Steps to the Destiny You Deserve

Amanda Steadman

© 2013 Published by **Amanda Steadman**

All Rights Reserved. No part of this publication may be reproduced in any form or by any means, including scanning, photocopying, or otherwise without prior written permission of the copyright holder.

First Printing, 2013

Printed Internationally.

Liability Disclaimer

By reading this document, you assume all risks associated with using the advice given below, with a full understanding that you, solely, are responsible for anything that may occur as a result of putting this information into action in any way, and regardless of your interpretation of the advice.

You further agree that our company cannot be held responsible in any way for the success or failure of your business as a result of the information presented below. It is your responsibility to conduct your own due diligence regarding the safe and successful operation of your business if you intend to apply any of our information in any way to your business operations.

Terms of Use

You are given a non-transferable, "personal use" license to this product. You cannot distribute it or share it with other individuals.

Also, there are no resale rights or private label rights granted when purchasing this document. In other words, it's for your own personal use only.

CONNECT TO AUTHENTIC SUCCESS: 7 STEPS TO THE DESTINY YOU DESERVE

Learn how to get what you want using easy, proven and tested success strategies you can implement instantly!

Bonus Resources Tool Kit included with this book at
www.amandasteadman.com/bonuses

Table of Contents

LIABILITY DISCLAIMER	3
TERMS OF USE	3
DEDICATION	**10**
ACKNOWLEDGEMENTS	**11**
PRAISE	**13**
AUTHORS NOTE	**17**
INTRODUCTION	**21**
WHAT ARE GOAL SETTING AND AUTHENTIC SUCCESS?	21
GOAL SETTING	21
AUTHENTIC SUCCESS	21
HOW TO USE THIS BOOK	**25**
WHAT IS IN IT FOR YOU?	**32**
YOU ARE PROBABLY ALREADY DOING IT!	32
THE AFFIRMATION APPROACH	33
THE SUPER FOCUSED APPROACH	34
NOT EVERYONE WANTS TO BE A MILLIONAIRE	35
STEP 1. ME - WHAT DO YOU REALLY, REALLY WANT?	**37**
GETTING CLEAR ON WHAT YOU DO AND DO NOT WANT!	37
BREAKING THE GOALS DOWN	42
WHAT CATEGORIES DO YOUR INITIAL GOALS FALL INTO?	43

FOCUSING ON THE RIGHT AREAS FOR YOU 44
SHORT, MEDIUM AND LONG TERM GOALS 45
WHAT HAS STOPPED YOU FROM GETTING WHAT YOU WANT SO FAR? ... 45
THE POWER OF POSITIVE BELIEFS 46
GETTING RID OF YOUR BLOCKS 47

ACTION STATION – PART 1 48

RELEASING NEGATIVE EMOTIONS 48

ACTION STATION - PART 2 50

REVEALING THE TRUE YOU 50

SUMMARY OF CHAPTER 1 52

STEP 2. ACTING THE END STEP 53

YOUR VISION 53
WHO ARE YOUR ROLES MODELS AND MENTORS? 54
AUTHENTIC SUCCESS TRAITS 55
HOW TO LEARN FROM OTHER AUTHENTICALLY SUCCESSFUL INDIVIDUALS ... 56
MODELLING 56
LIFE IS NOT A DRESS REHEARSAL 58
WHY AM I HERE? 59
WHEN THE GOING GETS TOUGH 60
LIFE CHALLENGES ARE TURNING POINTS 61
HAVE YOU HAD YOUR WAKE-UP CALL YET? 62

SUMMARY OF CHAPTER 2 66

STEP 3. GOAL PATH STRATEGY (GPS) 67

YOUR FLIGHT COORDINATES	67
TURNING CHALLENGES INTO OPPORTUNITIES	68
DO NOT WORRY ABOUT BEING PERFECT JUST BE HAPPY!	69

ACTION STATION – PART 1   72

YOUR H.E.A.R.T. ♥ SYSTEM	73
RESULTS FROM USING PRESENT TENSE AND TRUSTING	75
YOUR OWN TECHNIQUES	76
WHAT IF YOU MISS A DEADLINE?	80

ACTION STATION – PART 2   83

EXAMPLE: MY ♥ GOALS SHEET:	84

SUMMARY OF CHAPTER 3   90

STEP 4. I AM MAKING IT HAPPEN   91

SCHEDULING	91
MAKING IT HAPPEN VERSUS WAITING FOR IT TO HAPPEN	95
MOTIVATION VERSUS INSPIRATION	96
WHEN IT IS NOT GOING ACCORDING TO PLAN	98

ACTION STATION   99

BITE SIZE PLAN (BSP)	101

GOING THE DISTANCE   103

STAYING ON TRACK	104

SUMMARY OF CHAPTER 4 107

STEP 5. MIND OVER MATTER 108

MIND MECHANICS 108
How to get in the 'Flow' 110
Results from letting the 'Attachment' go 111
What is My Secret? 112
You Do Deserve It! 112
What other methods can you use to get your mind to produce results for you? 113

ACTION STATION 125

Frequency of Immersion 126

SUMMARY OF CHAPTER 5 127

STEP 6. YOUR POWER TEAM 128

What is a Power Team? 129
Resistance 132

ACTION STATION 134

Example Power Team Chart: 134

MY KEY POWER TEAM PEOPLE 135

SUMMARY OF CHAPTER 6 136

STEP 7. ON PURPOSE	**137**
BEING ON PURPOSE IS LIKE BEING IN FIRST CLASS	138
ACTION STATION	**140**
STEP 8. LOVE THE CHOCOLATE EFFECT – BONUS CHAPTER!	**143**
ACTION STATION	**146**
AUTHENTIC SUCCESS AGREEMENT	146
SOME MORE TIPS BEFORE YOU GO:	**150**
WHAT ARE YOUR NEXT STEPS TO SUCCESS & HAPPINESS?	**152**
INVITATION TO WORK WITH AMANDA	**152**
CONTACT AMANDA	**154**
FREE BONUS RESOURCES TOOL KIT – @WWW.AMANDASTEADMAN.COM/BONUSES	**155**
ABOUT THE AUTHOR	**156**

Dedication

To my Mum and Dad who taught me 'I could do anything I put my mind to' and my gorgeous family, Franck, Ava and Rosie

♥

Acknowledgements

Where do I start? To my parents who gave me a sound, loving childhood and the opportunity to always do what I wanted to do. To my mum, for showing me how to be an entrepreneur, independent and strong as well as the important fact that in life, people and love are more important than money or material possessions. To my dad, for showing me how to be organised and find a sensible solution to a problem (in a calm, controlled manner), as well as always being there for me. To my sister, Alison, for showing me how important life is and how emotionally strong a human can be. To my wonderful husband Franck, who puts up with me and my creative nature and my gorgeous daughters who teach me every day about the power of now and selflessness. To all of my extended family Lesley, Adam, Lally, Tony, Amy, Pat and clan, I have learned from all of you. I love you all x

To Mrs Rouse from Innsworth Junior School, you grew my creative loves of writing, art and the power of imagination. To all my other teachers and tutors over the years and mentors within the personal development realm who have given me the courage and tools to get where I am today, particularly Brian Tracy, Eckhart Tolle, Tony Robbins, Louise Hay, Wayne Dyer, Deepak Chopra, Marianne Williamson, Christine Kloser, Bob Proctor, Peggy McColl, Laura Berman-Fortgang, Michelle Whaite, Clinton Swaine, Denise Michaels, Dan Hall, Kathleen Gage, Bobby Gill, Adam Shaw, Jo Rose, Heidi Clingen to mention a few!

To all my wonderful friends, clients and fellow creatives around the world, without you, my life would not be the same and I look forward to continuing to illuminate the world with your gifts, knowledge and presence. You all ROCK!

A special kiss going out to Christine de la Cruz, fellow writer and mom whose beautiful soul has passed into the next room. x

This book is a combination of facts about Amanda Steadman's private and professional life and techniques she has used to dramatically improve her own life as well as all her clients. Some names of clients have been changed to protect confidentiality as requested.

♥

Praise

"This wonderful, inspiring book takes you by the hand and walks you through every step you need to take to live an extraordinary life."

Brian Tracy, International Best Selling Author, *Change Your Thinking, Change Your Life* and 52 other titles, 2011 Lifetime Achievement Award- National Academy of Best-Selling Authors.

"Connect to Authentic Success is a must read. Amanda shares with you all her secrets from despair to success and how you can avoid mistakes that lead to stress, dissatisfaction and lack of fulfillment. Follow her step-by-step formula that will lead you to the happiness and confidence you will experience by claiming your true destiny."

Peggy McColl, "The Best Seller Maker", New York Times Best-Selling Author

"If you are struggling with feelings of overwhelm, doubt and frustration, this book is for you. By following Amanda's 7 Step formula in Connect to Authentic Success, you will discover what truly makes you tick and how to maximize your authenticity by becoming MORE of who you already are!"

Christine Kloser, "The Transformation Catalyst", Three-Time Award Winning Author

"Playing by the old school rules is a thing of the past. Today we are able to create our life according to who we are called to be. In Connect to Authentic Success, author Amanda Steadman takes readers on a journey of self-discovery. Amanda combines one's practical self with their visionary self. Using effective goal setting to lay the foundation, she shows how right action is essential to one's success.

A great read for anyone who is looking for clear direction for their life."

Kathleen Gage, Business Strategist, Author, Speaker - Power Up For Profits

"I have had the experience of joint venturing with Amanda, as well as endorsing this book. She attracts an awesome crowd of individuals to work with. Her book is an extension of this and she provides practical solutions to some of the biggest challenges facing many people at the moment. This book will not only inspire you, but give you specific actionable ways to maximize your personal potential and make your life and business work for you."

Daniel Hall, Author, Speaker, Lawyer and Online Product Expert

"Anyone interested in carving their path to success needs Amanda's roadmap! Finding your way has never been easier. You will be delighted with the warm and real approach to leveraging the formula that connects your dreams of accomplishment to the satisfying life you choose to live. This should be a must read for everyone seeking success in their own life!"

Lil Roy, VP Strategic Planning, MRI Network

"We've all heard of the importance of setting goals but how many of us really know how to effectively set goals in a way that we can both achieve them and enrich our lives? In Connect to Authentic Success, Amanda takes us on a journey to a deeper place within ourselves as we identify our goals and dreams and then harness the power of her proven formula for achieving them. This book provides inspiration, motivation, and hope for anyone interested in achieving success, and achieving their dreams."

D'vorah Lansky, M.Ed. Bestselling Author of *Book Marketing Made Easy*

"If you have a passion to succeed on your terms, your way – you must read this book! Amanda takes you gently by the hand, providing practical "action stations" to help you create a schedule for your success. You move forward and get what you want. Finally! These aren't the same hashed over and over platitudes you find in other books. Amanda lays out a doable, kind-hearted plan to get you where you want to go – not by "white knuckling" yourself through and toughing it out, but by showing you the step-by-step secrets to putting your own support and resources in place, and, taking a genuine journey to authentic success."

Denise Michaels, Author of the Business Bestseller, "Testosterone-Free Marketing"

"If you want to read a book that inspires you and gives you clear practical tools to transform your life into one of less stress, more fulfillment, less confusion to more clarity and love; Amanda gives this to you, and more, in 'Connect to Authentic Success.' She comes from authenticity herself and with her stories and guidance (even with all the personal development experience I have!) Amanda has enabled me to have a clearer vision, an inspired heart and reminds me just how much I have to offer – simply as the awesome, authentic me!"

Adam Shaw, "The Heart Guy", Author & Speaker, Heart Wellbeing Ltd

"Finally, there is a book on success written from the soul. Start in your heart and work your way to those goals that will inspire you and make you happy. Amanda deserves all the success in her life and now **leaves clues;** she shares her secrets with those willing to read the book and take the action. Be the star in your own story!"

Bobby Gill, Writer, Internet Genius & Super Supporter, UK

"What an amazing and inspirational book for anyone who feels like there is something more for them, but cannot identify what it is. This book couldn't come at a better time—a time when more people are looking for authentic success that is driven by their passions."

Jill McKellan, Professional Ghostwriter and Author, USA

Authors Note

"Life is not a dress rehearsal so get up, dress up, and show up on your own life's stage!"

- Amanda Steadman

Goal setting and authentic success are not something new however; my approach to them has changed dramatically over the last fifteen years. My aim was always to get closer to my core, to enable my clients to feel authentically happy and successful. Now I understand what authentic success really means. It is a success from the inside out. Many of the tools you will learn in this book will ignite external actions but your focus on how each step 'feels' to you, and if it instils passion, will be clues as to whether it resonates with the 'true you'. For some of us we intrinsically know we are on a path to authentic success, for others we need a lending hand and a refocusing of those internal guides, particularly through 'meditation' or 'quiet time' in order to connect with our inner success before we experience it on the outside. The practical exercises and stories in this book will enable YOU to get started right away.

I have been working with the concept of goal setting all my life. When I look at my life today and how happy I am, I can attribute much of it to this wonderful skill. Some people say 'goal setting' is an "old idea" or is no longer a relevant process. I disagree! It is such an important part of my life today. If your idea of goal setting is sitting down and writing a list of goals that you will never look at again, let us change that! Goal setting is so much more! It is the secret to figuring out what you want from this life and why you want it. With goal setting, you will be happy with what you achieved but more importantly, you will be thrilled with **WHO YOU have become!**

I credit goal setting with much of my personal and professional success. That is why I am so passionate about sharing my techniques with you. A popular version of success is to have material wealth, fame, and the externally focussed acquisitions. The new version of success and mentality that is growing is, actually **I want to 'feel good', I want to spend time with my family, I want a career that makes me happy, I want to have a healthy body, and I want to grow spirituality.** Do any of these resonate with you? Do you find you are already perhaps successful but something is missing? These goals are more inwardly focused and based around emotions that you will experience around particular events and lifestyle. The H.E.A.R.T Goals system we created will enable you to get clear on where you want to go and what you want to experience.

Going for my dreams was not always easy, but I am grateful to say that I have personal and professional fulfilment that I never dreamed was possible. To encourage you, I want you to know that my life today has been created by a series of goals. For example, I am married to a gorgeous Frenchman, Franck (I wrote a list and life script for my ideal partner in July 2002) and we have two beautiful, healthy daughters Ava Jane and Esmé Rose (I call her Rosie and both daughters appeared after extensive visualisation and being on vision boards). I do the work I want to do. We live near a beach, and I eat out at restaurants whenever I want to, I serve many clients throughout my business, and I am earning income through this work and other investments.

Does it sound too good to be true? Believe me, if it were not for goal setting, I would not be where I am right now! That is why I am very grateful and I want YOU to have the success that you yearn for, too, not just material success but authentic success from a place of true fulfilment.

So I decided to take gather my courage and pour out my heart and secrets into this book. My goal is for you to know HOW to make this work for you, to give yourself PERMISSION, and to REMIND you that you DESERVE a happy, fulfilling life. Once you start reading and COMMITTING to doing the exercises or as I call them **'Action Stations'** in this book, things WILL CHANGE positively for YOU!

I cannot wait for you to Connect to YOUR Authentic Success Today.

To your health, wealth and success

Amanda x

Remember to get your Bonus Resources Tool Kit included with this book at www.amandasteadman.com/bonuses

"You already have all the answers within you. You just need to connect to how amazing you already are; and how your wonderful, natural gifts are waiting to be used in the world today!"

Amanda Steadman
_____

Introduction

What are Goal Setting and Authentic Success?

> *"Success is the progressive realization of a worthy idea."*
>
> **Earl Nightingale**

Goal Setting

It is amazing that only 5% of the world population sets goals and you are about to become one of them! Even though the practice of goal setting has been around for centuries, few people practice this skill knowingly. Goal setting is the realisation of your worthy idea.

Authentic Success

> *"Authentic Success comes from the inside out, unless you know what truly makes you happy, the external success is unlikely to fulfil you"*
>
> **Amanda Steadman**

The majority of today's achievers, from the pop world to the sports world, have a goal or plan of some sort that they take action on every day. This book will reveal many of the techniques that these successful people use and that have worked for my clients and I. Goal setting is a very personal journey and I want to share mine with you, so you can learn fast how to replicate the results, feel successful and be happy!

A few blessed individuals know at a very early age exactly what they want to do with their lives: Richard Branson, Barack Obama, Mozart, and Madonna, to name a few. For many of us, this journey can take a little longer and it can be years before we discover what actually makes us come alive, what fills us with passion and spurs us on to the goals and dreams that we set for ourselves. Authentic success comes from the heart, a place where you can be truly happy, where you are being yourself and using all your natural talents and abilities.

Goal setting and success in their basic form are as Earl Nightingale describes above, decide what you want most, commence the steps to get there and engage passion to propel you to reach your desires.

Success is also the fulfilling of those desires. The more you progress through this book, the clearer you will be about what success actually means to you. I have found that over time, and as you move into different stages of your life, your definition of success may change dramatically. Whichever way it goes, do not beat yourself up if it does not always go according to 'your' plan. If you listen to your intuition and your heart, it will help you identify what path to take as well as using the tools in this book. Once you get clarity on what 'Authentic Success' means for you, all the steps to take will be laid out for you. This will be the foundation, as well as the first chapter for you to start revealing the 'true you'. Congratulations for having the courage to get this far. I am already proud of you!

Just writing this book was a HUGE GOAL of mine. I kept thinking, "What do I know? What if my family reads this? When will I ever get it finished? How long should it be? Have I said enough? Does it have enough actions steps in it, because I really 'want' people to DO SOMETHING WITH THIS INFORMATION, not just leave it on their shelf".

Therefore, no matter what your version of success is, you are bound to second guess yourself, there will be periods of doubt, there will be periods where you may not believe you can do it and others around you may try to back this up. Listen to your heart and follow it, do not let anyone steal your dreams and be prepared to overcome those obstacles that may come your way. I will be with you every step of the way!

> *"If you just set out to be liked, you would be prepared to compromise on anything at any time, and you would achieve nothing."*
> **Margaret Thatcher**

Despite all these obstacles, when you start to **connect to your 'inner wisdom', your intuition,** you will start to choose goals that will enable you to feel genuinely successful as you are completing them and **not JUST at the END**. You can choose to celebrate every step, as you get closer. You do not have to WAIT to feel good. If they do not make you feel 'good', they probably are not the right goals for you.

How to Use this Book

"You can give people all the information they need to succeed, but if you don't have the right attitude, if you don't want it enough – it's not going to happen for you"

Amanda Steadman

This book is compiled of the most important factors effecting goal setting that you need to know to progress. Alongside this will be √ **Action Stations** that you are encouraged to do to make immediate use of the information and get your conscious and subconscious brain engaged in finding solutions into how you will get where you want to be!

There are seven steps that you need to follow that are detailed in each chapter of the book. I have written it in the easiest way to digest, and you can apply the Action Stations at the end of each chapter that are there to guide you. You can go from Chapter One to Seven, however, if there is a certain section that jumps out at you that you want to dive into – go ahead.

The first chapter focuses on getting you to clarity, clarity on what you do and do not want, clarity on what you are prepared to undertake to realise your desires in life. It will take you through various questions so narrow down your focus to those areas that are most important to you. The areas of life you want to work on are also discussed so you can get your creative juices going on how you want to style your life and enhance what you already have.

Chapter Two starts to engage your imagination and brain to start thinking about how your life can be by visualising your desired result. If you start with the end result you want in your mind, you are putting a pin in the board; you are marking where you want to go. Now your mind has to come up with a solution, your subconscious has something to aim for. It also serves as a reminder that your time on this planet (depending on your beliefs!) This human body is finite so whatever you are here to do, seize the day! You are unique, with your own talents and abilities so your ultimate authentic success will have you realising your true purpose here. These Chapters will assist you through this process.

In Chapter Three - it starts to get even more practical as you begin to plan some of the markers and actions you may need to take between your current position and your final destination. You will get specific examples of how you can start to take your goals, break them down into bite-size chunks and begin to take action. This is where I go through the HEART goal system with you. There are HEART Goal Sheets for you to fill in or use the links provided to download and print your free copies that accompany the book.

Chapter Four - great, you are clear on what you want, you have an idea of your plan ahead and you have put it into your HEART Goal Fun Sheets. Now you have to be super focussed in order to 'schedule' it all in order to make it happen, to make it real. It is very easy to make a list of goals in your diary then forget about them (which many of us do at New Year!) I want you to be different. I want you to progress, to get what you deserve – so this section is 'key' to making sure you are 'making things happen' and holding yourself accountable. I also know that not everything goes according to plan, so that will be covered too! No need to be perfect in everything, the aim is to be happy - right?

Chapter Five - this is one of my favourite parts of setting outcomes and imagining what you can truly achieve in your life. Our mind is an amazing phenomenon. It was only when I started seeing the results of vision boards, (goals in a visual format – more on this later), written detailed goals and more importantly, quiet accepting expectation, that I witnessed the power of my own mind working hand in hand with destiny. I endeavour to open your mind to the content of this book and its contents. I go into detail on techniques that I use with clients and give many examples. There are also links to online examples and audios, so you can benefit from the book and live examples to use straight away.

Chapter Six – This book is a great companion for your journey, from examples, to sheets, audios, and case studies to ensure your success. One essential element of achievement you will find behind many successful people, is that they have a team supporting them from family to coaches, mentors and mastermind groups. In order to get to where you want to go, your network of support will be there to see you through those times where it may be challenging. Where you need to bounce your ideas off someone who understands you completely, when you need someone to hold you to a higher standard who will not let you quit! This is your Action Team, your own 'A' team! 'A' stands for accountability, action, achievement and authenticity! With them, the path is a little more smooth and a whole lot more fun!

For many years I struggled to progress because I wanted to prove how independent and strong I was. I struggled to delegate in my business because I wanted to control all elements, which consequently ran into my private life! Over recent years, I have witnessed the power of mastermind groups, coaching and mentoring. As a successful coach, mentor and trainer myself, it took me quite a while to put my hand up and say," I think I need a little help and guidance here!" No matter how good you are at what you do, there is always someone more experienced, wiser and possibly more 'successful than you are at the moment. Before, I used to be envious of these people. Now I reach out to them and ask them to mentor me, I interview them and I look to add value to them. Recently I put a couple of my mentors in touch with each other, as I saw great joint venture potential. I go into detail in this chapter, because I wish your path to be faster and easier than mine. This chapter will show you how to put your power team or dream team together and leverage them to faster success.

Chapter Seven - This is a chapter to enable you to springboard to your authentic success as it is about **PURPOSE!** These previous chapters will excavate what you probably already know, but have not had the courage to listen to yet. Your life blueprint is waiting for you! You will be given specific probing questions to uncover some of the answers as to what you are here for and what you are supposed to be doing with your wonderful life! This is an essential part of connecting with your AUTHENTIC SUCCESS. This is one of the most important parts of figuring out what success means to you and what makes your heart sing!

Chapter Eight (Bonus Chapter) – The Chocolate Effect talks about getting into a new comfort zone. Goal setting has definitely grown on me. As a coach and mentor to hundreds of clients, it has been my pleasure to see individuals blossom and truly find their destiny in the world. It is a skill that I believe gets a whole lot easier with time and the process for me has become even more effortless as my mind tunes into that magical frequency that makes things happen. It is a continuous process, so this chapter deals with how you can best master the procedure, and as you start to see the results of your motivation, re-setting and reaching for your dreams becomes positively infectious.

Some areas of this book may be uncomfortable to you because it is new, so I encourage you, with all my heart, to start using these techniques, to believe in them and the fact that you actually deserve great results. I have every faith in you! If I can do it, you can too.

Even if you have set goals before, there will always be something that surfaces that you may not have considered. So approach this with an open mind and potentially revisit some of those older goals!

For those of you that want to concentrate on a specific area – wealth, for example - you can complete the entire book with this focus. Whatever you focus on expands! You could breeze through all these pages and *not* do any of the exercises – but I KNOW you will get so much more if you apply yourself to every Action Station request. *"What you reap you will sow"* and I want YOU TO SUCCEED! So GO FOR IT!

What I will be covering in this book is a combination of knowledge from the "greats" of enriching human potential, my experiences, my clients, friends, mentors and other successful and wealthy individuals today and throughout history.

I talk about what I use daily and what has worked for my clients and me. These techniques really do WORK if you apply them in your own way and make the effort. This is why I am so passionate about this subject. Everyone needs to know this information. I am convinced it can work for everyone if each person puts forth the effort and trust in the process. You deserve the best in your life so do not sell yourself short! The fact that you are reading this book shows you are willing to take your life to the next level, you know you deserve more and that you are still searching for some of the answers you need to move forward. I look forward to assisting you to progress on your amazing journey!

Even if you are used to goal setting on a regular basis, you know that every endeavour you make to stimulate that amazing computer in your head is likely to pay off. The energy you are putting into this book is already starting to shift your focus towards more positive experiences.

For a more seasoned goal setter, I am probably preaching to the converted! For those of you who are new to these ideas, test them, play with them, and I promise you; even if you do *some* of these exercises on the following pages, things, people, and circumstances WILL change in your life. I have seen it happen repeatedly in my life, the life of my family and friends, and very importantly I have seen it happen to my clients!

Have a little faith, dive in and go for it 110% ... You will not regret it - and neither did all those other successful, wealthy and happy people that have gone before you. This is the time in your life to create your own story, your own 'Authentic Success'...so let us now begin….

Note that I will be using these terms interchangeably: God, the Universe, The Source, and Infinite Intelligence. Please use whatever works with YOUR belief system. I wish to show you what has worked for my clients and me, as you get closer to your 'authentic self' and the inner and outer success that is your birthright.

What is in it for you?

It totally depends on what you want from your life. Do you believe you deserve a fabulous life? Do you believe you can do work that fulfils you and are rewarded for it? Do you believe you can attract the ideal partner, have kids, build a business, and have the ideal figure? I have been setting goals at a conscious level for over fifteen years now (all of my life subconsciously!) and it never fails to astound me as to how the majority of them become a reality.

Even before I realized it as a little girl, I was a goal setter. For example, I was very good at saving money when I was very young. Even at 8 years old, I had a post office account and used to put any spare birthday or pocket money in there and by the time I was 11 years old it had become almost £2000 ($3000) and that was a lot of money in the 1980's. I was very much into Barbie Dolls and art back then, so I would set a financial goal to save enough to buy what I wanted, so some of the seeds were already sown.

You are probably already doing it!

The other area where I started setting goals and achieving them, was the Brownies and Girl Guides. These are organised groups for children to learn the qualities of communication, and leadership, developing skills you may not achieve at school. I was always a bit competitive and bossy (so said most of my teachers, and particularly Mrs Rouse when I was nine years old!) so the Girl Guides, especially, was a great opportunity for me, as I had to lead four to eight other girls in the 'patrol' (group) in events and meetings, motivating them to achieve their 'aptitude badges'. I loved 'earning' these. I would firstly decide, "Right I would like to get my first aid badge by this semester". I would then talk to the Guide Leader, tell them what I was planning and follow instructions on how to obtain the necessary skills. I would then be tested, pass and be presented with my prize: The badge. I loved that sense of achievement and pride once I had a new skill and could help others in the group achieve theirs.

The Affirmation Approach

As an adult, when I travelled around the world, I read Louise L Hay's 'Heal your Life' book and she has numerous 'affirmations' in it. I used these principles to create some of my own whilst globetrotting, for example 'I always have a free place to stay and 'I am looked after wherever I go'. Amazingly, I travelled solo for almost 2 years and nothing too sinister happened. In addition, for almost a year I had free accommodation, so I had proved that repetition and the power of belief could seriously manifest things. This period was where a sincere interest and passion for goal setting and personal development as an adult began.

Once I returned to the UK after my world travels, I ventured into the corporate world. I came home from Bangkok on the Sunday and found a job by the following Monday – at the hard-core end of 1990's business – SALES! I did not realise it was sales. I had done some work for a manager called Annabel in my summer holidays and because I had always done a good job, and was reliable, they hired me full time to talk to people on the phone. I thought "wow, they are going to pay me to talk to people, (one of my favourite pastimes!) I get a computer, a desk, and a budget for lunches, and drinks on a Friday. This is cool!" I had it made! My basic salary was low, but the commission was quite generous.

The Super Focused Approach

I started using Brian Tracy's (a successful sales and personal development expert) sales training to go from a new sales person to one of the top sales people in the territory (I go into more detail on this in the section 'Acting The End Step'). This was a more structured type of goal setting as I had specific sales targets to hit and I knew how many calls and visits I would need to make to reach my desired outcome. I also worked very hard, going the extra mile for clients and candidates, for which I was rewarded very well financially.

Therefore, we have discussed more examples of visualising a goal, deciding it was wanted, figuring out some of the steps required to get there, taking action and celebrating the achievement. In a way school and college assists with some of the skills associated with 'goal setting'. Although when we think of 'pure' goal setting it's more about what our heart DESIRES than things we 'have' to do. We will talk more about this later.

You just need to know that wherever you are in your life right now, you have all the skills and the desires you need to make the decision and start being willing to take some action! Your authentic success is not too far away!

Not everyone wants to be a millionaire

Not everyone is a "goal setter", not everyone wants to push himself or herself to a higher level, and that is ok! Everyone has his or her own journey. I have some clients who want to be a fantastic mom, partner, or be the best possible manager at work. Others want to write a book, become famous, help save the planet, or change the world. Everyone is different and each one sets their own goal in their own way. Always follow what feels right to you and let no-one dissuade you. There is EVERYTHING IN IT FOR YOU, IF YOU WANT IT ENOUGH! So let us start creating and getting clear about what YOU desire and who you want to be.

"Those who succeed have goals and people who have goals succeed."

Amanda Steadman
___

Step 1. ME - What do YOU Really, Really Want?

> *"Don't wait for everything to be perfect. Start from where you are, start from 'ideal' then believe that providence will move for YOU!"*
>
> **Amanda Steadman**

Getting Clear on What You Do and Do not Want!

Stop and ask anyone, "What do you really, really want in life?" and the responses generally fall into four categories:

- "I don't know what my goals are. What are goals again?"

- "I want to be a millionaire, rich, comfortable and not work anymore." (When you have the money, though, what else will make you get out of bed and see the world?)

- "I don't want to be poor, I don't want to be alone, I don't want to stay in my job and I don't want to be fat." (You may think, "Oh that's so negative!" However, if you do know what you DO NOT want, it is a start to working towards what you DO want.)

- "By 20__ I will have sold my company for £7million, be tithing 10% to a children's charity, fulfilled my dream of crossing the Atlantic, and be spending all the rest of my time with my wife, family and friends."

Which one are you? We work with individuals to get them clear on what they want. On most occasions, this part of the goal puzzle can be the most difficult. Once you are CLEAR on this – you can start to put the other parts of the puzzle together. It is not an overnight solution, it will take time to figure out what you want and they change with time too!

Getting Clear on What You Want Helps You To:

- **Work out what you really want.**

You are the only one who knows what you really want, and it is often not what you think.

In 2002, I set a goal that I wanted to become and Oscar Winning Actress. I started all the necessary plans to make it happen. At 31, it was going to be tricky to get into full time drama school, but what the heck, why not. My friends even bought me a fake Oscar Award to use in my visualisations! Over a few years, I worked very hard at acting. I followed the actor's path and went to drama school. I went to every audition possible and I worked on all types of film and TV sets for money, and sometimes for free just to get the experience. It was a very exciting, demanding time in my life. I had butterflies on film sets. I loved being involved and especially working with famous actors. On my last film, before I had my first daughter, I got to work with Dennis Quaid and Michael Sheen as a PA to Tony Blair in 'The Special Relationship'. It took me 6 years to get that far!

What happens when your big dream doesn't make you happy anymore?

At one point, I was running a full time business squeezed into part time to support the acting career, but I do not think that some of my tutors at my drama school really understood that. Unfortunately, I let attitudes towards me begin to dissipate my love for studying acting and then acting itself. I actually let it happen; in retrospect, I could have managed my emotions, and ego around it, much better. I can see that at the time they wanted to prepare us for the tough acting world ahead (It was one of the toughest industries I had ever worked in.) Instead, I lost the desire to be the actress that I yearned to be. I could have fought harder, I could have competed better with my acting colleagues, but my heart was just not following suit. My inner self had other plans for me. Despite the years, time, energy, the money and soul I had already invested into it. It was not for the fame; it definitely was not for the money (as most of my acting friends will tell you!). For me, one of the greatest rewards of acting was being 'in the moment', being that character, and being in that perfect 'zone'. The second part I loved was communicating a message, the emotions behind the story or the soul of the character I was portraying. It is quite ironic that I now convey powerful messages and emotions as 'myself' when speaking to my audiences!

Is there another message for you from destiny?

To 'be **an actress'** wasn't necessarily the big goal any more. The new vision became getting a message out to people that would move them emotionally through other mediums. I could have done it as an actress and I did for a while. Now I have found my passion – writing and communicating the message as myself! (Nevertheless, I do not see any reason why I could not star in a major motion picture. I am open to offers Mr Steven Spielberg and Mr Woody Allen!) It just shows that when destiny has a plan for you, there are many roads to the same dream! Are you starting to feel inspired yet?

The other part of acting that I enjoyed tremendously was getting up early, getting to a film location, connecting with other actors and being part of the buzz of a film being created around you. Knowing you are part of something bigger that will leave a legacy, move people emotionally and ideally communicate the director's vision! We will get you thinking and acting on the vision you are going to create for yourself. Now it is your turn to write your OWN script! How exciting!

Looking back I realise this was part of my journey. I started to do more speaking and more stage work within my business. Therefore, the acting was another stepping-stone closer to doing what I am here to do. Getting the message out there that you are fine the way you are, get on purpose and be happy! Find your authentic success and the destiny you deserve. This is one of the reasons for writing this book so you too can 'get' to happy! **You do not have to take as long as I did. You can get there right now by using this book!**

Clients (and many friends!) ask me to help them figure out what their next steps should be. They have an idea of what they think they want. By the time we have completed our sessions they have a completely new direction and the confidence to move forward into it. You will soon read some of the stories of my clients that highlight this point.

- **Get the motivation to put your plan into action.**

Since your goals will be personal and meaningful to you and based on what success truly means to you, you will be motivated to achieve it, that is, if there is a big enough WHY behind it. When I say WHY I mean the WHY behind the goal. Everyone would like more money, but what are you going to DO with it once you get it? Some clients want to spend more time with their families, some clients want a bigger house, some clients want to do some well-earned travel, and some clients want to re-invest the money into cash-generating investments for their kids. Whatever your WHY is, it usually determines how much effort you are willing to put in and in most cases how authentically successful you will be.

- **Work out a plan to help you achieve what you really want**.

There is no point in having a great goal if you are not motivated or inspired enough to get there. We will cover this later on in the book, step-by-step.

- **Determine your direction, your starting place.**

They are your road maps to success (that is, what YOU consider to be success), your life's plan, your personal guide to the future.

- **Keep track of where you are going by helping you focus on the big picture.**

This ensures you do not lose your way. It is easy to get distracted by life's obstacles, so this process will assist you in focusing your time and energy in the right direction.

Breaking the Goals Down

Here are some examples of different goal forms.

- How to improve your current skills, whether they are focused on career tasks or life skills such as budgeting?

- How to beat old habits like smoking, and developing better ones like exercise and healthy eating habits.

- How to develop a new skill, perhaps you have always wanted to learn a new language, how to dance, or how to play a musical instrument.

- How to produce an outcome or achieve your dream. It could be starting a company, finding a partner, creating wealth or a achieving a career goal.

- How to create more TIME to do MORE things you enjoy doing and spending more time with people you care about.

- How to be a more confident, centred, human being, feeling fulfilled in all you do. Knowing who you truly are and attracting the destiny you deserve.

What categories do your initial goals fall into?

Here are some of the categories you can consider:

- Personal
- Financial
- Mental
- Family
- Career
- Physical
- Spiritual
- Community & Global

When I first started consciously setting goals, many of mine were about 'having' rather than being for example:

- Having the status of the best sales person

- Having an $80,000 a year salary

- Having a 5 bedroom detached house

- Having an intelligent, driven partner

- Having the means to be able to buy from any designer shop I wanted

- Having access to global travel

Over the last 15 years, they have become more about being authentic and purpose driven:

- Being a transformational leader - fulfilling my purpose as a communicator of the message that Life IS as AWESOME as you want it to be and here are the tools to make it so

- Being in my own space

- Being with friends

- Being with people I love via more holidays/vacations!

- Being able to be myself and using new mediums such as products/courses/speaking engagements/radio shows to spread my message

Focusing on the right areas for you

There is nothing wrong with any of the goals above. It depends where you are on your journey. Some of us have a negative feeling towards having a lot of money. I have also seen that this does not serve anyone. The more value you add to other people the more reward you deserve. You are making a difference no matter what field you are in. If it comes from the heart and you are being authentically yourself, success by your definition WILL find you!

What I found with clients is that sometimes it takes time to excavate what is already there. We're so busy being busy, moms, dads, entrepreneurs, writers, wives, teachers, that we don't take the time to really think about key life questions such as who am I, what do I want and what am I are here for? As you work though the action stations in this book diligently, the answers will start to surface. You will be excavating your path to authentic success.

As I go through these types of exercises with clients, they experience similar realizations and intuitively we come to the same conclusions. It is always good to feel you are covering a goal in each category. However, for countless numbers of my clients, they tend to focus on their key challenge areas first and work outwards. Focus on whatever you feel you need to address at this point in your life and what correlates with your goal timings.

Short, Medium and Long Term Goals

As well as the above categories, there tend to be three types of time frames for goals: Short, Medium and Long Term. The larger and more ambitious goals may be in your Long Term vision. Nonetheless, when you start to work backwards, there will be numerous actions that will fall into the other two time bands.

What Has Stopped You from Getting What You Want So Far?

Go back to the goals you have written down so far. Many of us do know what we want, but we do not know how to get there or that we are holding ourselves back through what we call **limiting beliefs**. These are usually negative false thoughts we hold in our subconscious that usually talk to us! For example 'I'm not qualified enough', 'You can't do that!', 'You're not strong enough.' The list goes on. Do you recognise any of those?

Even seasoned goal setters have to get rid of those negative messages too. It is a constant task like cleaning out those cobwebs in your house! We look at these thoughts in a different way and do not focus on them! Do not beat yourself up when you have them, as a human being, unless you are super enlightened, you will hear thoughts coming in and out. If they are negative, acknowledge them and then let them go right back out again. Chase them with some of the positive affirmations we will cover soon. Affirmations are only one way of doing this and a good start. The more you work with your mind and heart, the stronger your skills will be to 'handle' the energy associated with these beliefs and thoughts. Whatever may be holding you back in terms of negative thoughts; we will tackle this in the next action station.

The Power of Positive Beliefs

There is a successful millionaire named Brian Tracy who, on one of his CD's, tells us he repeated to himself hundreds of times a day "I like myself; I like myself" because he had a huge lack of confidence when he started out in sales.

He soon built his confidence up enough to become the best sales persons in the company by combining this technique with the goal to be No.1 in sales. He went on to become a multimillionaire while helping millions of people achieve their goals too!

I learned about Brian Tracy in 1998, and applied most of his goal setting and sales techniques to the sales role I was in at the time. I bought his cassettes and turned my car into a University on Wheels! I listened, repeated the information and got superb results.

At the time, friends, family and colleagues thought I was crazy. However, within six months I had increased my income by 40% and become one of the top sales people in the region! I was focused, determined, and consistent. I believed it would happen. I went on to be even more successful in other areas and have achieved hundreds of goals that I have set since then. And so can YOU! Over time, I have created my own versions of these types of tools and used them with clients to achieve their success a little easier.

Let us look at what we have discussed in this chapter and ask yourself the following questions. Be honest and open with yourself, this is not a competition! Give yourself permission to clear out the closet and move on to exactly what you truly deserve. The more you give of yourself to these exercises the more you will get back.

Getting Rid of Your Blocks

In this action station, you are going to create your own positive affirmations in order to change a belief and consequent behaviour. All the statements are created in the present tense. This works on your conscious, but more importantly your subconscious mind as the latter accepts these as 'instructions'. It is imperative that you are aware of the power of these negative beliefs on a daily basis and that you develop the habit to replace them with positive ones. The first part of the action station will assist you. There is also an exercise on releasing negative emotions – which tend to be the culprits behind the blocks!

Action Station – Part 1

Releasing Negative Emotions

The first part of your 'Action Station' is to start eliminating those blocks to your success. Then you will move onto the second part including getting specific about what you DO want in the next set of exercises.

Let us get clear about what you want to let go of first. Grab a pen and paper, fold the paper in two and list any negative sayings that you know you repeat in your head or get in the way. Which ones stand out the most, or you think hold you back the most?

Whatever they are, write the opposite to them on the other side of the same page and then cross out the negative one. Type up or print out the list of POSITIVE statements and put them somewhere you will see them regularly. It speeds up the process if you repeat it aloud too. (If you have not done this before it does feel a bit odd to start with but you get used to it and start to see the results):

I am educated enough to do exactly what I want.

I can do it and I am confident.

I am wealthy.

I am worthy and charge what I am worth

I am a successful entrepreneur/author

I am knowledgeable enough to start

There are also four key negative emotions that it is best to 'release.' By that I mean that as soon as you start to feel them. Say in your head "I appreciate you and now I release you, and a little bit more, and a little bit more." What you should find is that the emotion dissipates. If not keep going until it does. It's a simple and effective technique. Emotions are energy that needs to be released. So move that kind of energy on and OUT!

If you look back at your answers to Action Station one your goals or the achievement of them will generally elicit an EMOTION that you want to experience. Most of us want to experience fulfilment, joy, gratitude, a feeling of PURPOSE. Look at your goals again.

What emotions do you desire? Focus on what makes you HAPPY, what gives you a feeling of fulfilment. It's very easy to get carried away with 'material' type goals, however once you start on this journey to discovering more about the power within, you will start to see that the true power of goal setting and the emotions you want to achieve are not as far away as you think. As the Good Witch Glenda says in the Wizard of Oz – 'You had the answer with you all along'.

Action Station - Part 2

Revealing the True You

Then next part of the 'Action Station' for this chapter is to start uncovering what you want most in your life now and in the future.

Answer the questions below to uncover what is most important to you and could form the foundation of the authentic goals you will set.

1. **What are you NOT happy with in your life right now? What do you most want to change?**

2. **On a scale of 1-10 how happy are you with your life? (10 being "blissed out!")**

3. **What would have to happen for you to take it to 11 out of 10?**

4. **What do you like/love most about your life right now?**

5. **What do you want to be/do or have this year, two years and five years from now?**

6. What do you want to earn, per month net by year-end/within the next 12 months?

7. What is the emotion you most want to experience on a regular basis? Is it fulfilment, happiness, security, peace of mind? The emotion(s) you are seeking will be a real clue as to what desires are truly from your heart and others you have gathered along the way. They will also be indicators of what goals will be prioritised first.

8. What kind of person do you want to become? Who you will be when you feel authentically successful?

How well did you answering the questions? **Once you have answered these questions, it will give you a clearer picture of where you are now and where you want to be. Are there any gaps? Are there any answers that have surprised you?**

Well done, you have started to eliminate some of those negative beliefs you have and have started to get your subconscious working on what you DO want. You have completed Chapter One!

The next chapter will look at envisioning that 'End Step', which usually elicits those favourite emotions that you want to experience consistently. You are already starting to design your now and your future. How exciting!

Summary of Chapter 1

- ✓ You will have learned the power of clarity and decision making.

- ✓ You will have started to craft your initial goals.

- ✓ You will have started to define the categories of life that are most important to you.

- ✓ You will have started to eliminate old conditioned programming.

- ✓ You are now open to accepting new positive thinking and energy.

- ✓ Watch the world change around you as you start implementing each of these steps.

- ✓ You have activated your subconscious mind to work towards what you want, rather than what you don't want!

Step 2. Acting the End Step

> *"Cherish your visions and your dreams as they are the children of your soul; the blueprints of your ultimate achievements."*
>
> *Napoleon Hill*

Your Vision

On your goal-setting journey, I highly advise that you read much more on this subject. This book is to ignite your interest and give you a taste of what is possible on a much grander scale. I have learned tremendous amounts from individuals such as Tony Robbins, Eckhart Tolle, Anita Roddick, Bob Proctor, Marianne Williamson, Wayne Dyer to name a few!

They all have visions and an idea of what the 'Big Picture' is. They start with the end goal step in mind and work backwards. They all started small, took action, found mentors, built their teams and fulfilled their dreams. Eckhart was slightly different, success found him. We will investigate this as you move through the chapters. What end step or vision do you have in mind?

Who are your Roles Models and Mentors?

Goal Setting and Success Strategies were two of my favourite subjects to teach whilst I was in corporate life. I was Head of Performance Development for a global recruitment company – headquartered in Cleveland, Ohio. I was based in their Windsor office in the UK (about 5 minutes' walk from the Queens Castle Residence and a few minutes from where Prince Harry and Prince William went to school. I saw both of them in their school uniforms once). Doug Bugie and James Caan, two extremely successful entrepreneurs with very big visions of what a business could become, started the original company. They also knew how to develop their employees particularly well and invested large amounts in training. They reaped the rewards after many years of hard work and both are multimillionaires now. James went on to become a Dragon in the UK's business TV Series Dragons Den, where entrepreneurs pitch their business ideas to the millionaires for their investment of time and cash and a percentage of the profits.

I was fortunate to have a boss within one of their companies, Lil Roy, a charismatic Texan who is an inspiration leader and a superb example of authentic success. She assisted me to grow within my corporate role and to launch a brand new division within it. As we travelled together I got to see how she operated, her use of words, her way of managing heated discussions! She was my mentor and I still apply her advice today. I never forget the day she said to me "You have leadership potential Amanda and I will manage you to greatness," and she did.

My director of training was also an avid goal setter. He would write his daily, normally with his Montblanc Pen and Journal!

Much of our management and leadership material was based on solid personal development principles. I trained hundreds of consultants and many franchise owners in this knowledge and launched two new divisions in my time there. I was fortunate, as I learned how to succeed in business via the mistakes and accomplishments of the franchise owners, whilst building my confidence in launching a new business. I went on to develop a consultancy using much of this tried and tested material, which produced the best results for our programmes and clients. One of my favourite sayings is 'Success leaves clues.' By following specific steps with the right attitude and heart you will become successful. Ensure you choose whom you follow and their definition of success wisely. Ask yourself; are they truly an example of authentic success that resonates with me?

Authentic Success Traits

If you look at the top 5% of 'successful people, they have particular traits, ways of doing things, a can-do attitude and many of them share in books, on TV, when they speak HOW they actually did it. These are your clues to success; pick someone from your chosen field. Have you noticed that the conversation usually includes the words 'vision', 'goals', 'dreams', 'desires' as well. They use phrases such as, "I worked at it," "I practiced," "I put my mind to it," "I trusted," "I took it step by step," "the opportunity presented itself". They DID and THOUGHT and FELT certain things in order to reach their goals. They knew already in their mind and heart what their 'END STEP' was then they worked backwards to figure out how they could do it and if anyone had already done it before.

How to learn from other Authentically Successful Individuals

Last century Andrew Carnegie commissioned a young man called Napoleon Hill to study success. Napoleon spent many of his years interviewing successful people of the time. They mentioned that on many occasions they would take the paths of people who had succeeded before them. They took the advice of mentors, visionaries who had already achieved the success they wanted to and without compromising what they stood for.

If you talk to these individuals, their success is an extension of WHO they are. They are authentically themselves and have attracted the right teams to work with them. Richard Branson is one of my favourite examples, he is a creative 'think-outside-the-box', risk-taking person, but his founding partners were more 'logical' left-brained and less risk averse in their approach. Together they built Virgin group of companies to be what it is today. Richard is a great example of being authentically successful. That is not to say he is perfect, he has made some mistakes like all of us. The point I am making is that he stays true to what he believes is right for him and his companies. He knows what it takes to succeed by his **own** definition.

Modelling

If you want to be a successful author, you find out who is a flourishing author in your field, you read their books, you study their background, you study their habits, the way they write, you may even attend their seminars or training programmes where they SHARE with YOU, HOW THEY DID IT. Then you simply APPLY those steps and start moving forward. This way you can leverage all their effort, time and knowledge as you consequently speed up your success story.

This is referred to as 'modelling.' This concept suggests that if you model one of these individuals you can create similar success – a little like the concept of franchising in the business world. There is already a blueprint and you can follow its instructions. This does not mean you lose yourself, your values or your unique gifts and become a copy of your mentor, just that you use their tools and avoid the mistakes they made.

You can still use examples or successful 'models' within your arena and build it YOUR WAY. This is what Mark Zuckerberg, one of the creators of Facebook did. There were already similar platforms and he studied what other Internet geniuses had done and improved it. At the time of writing Facebook is a global phenomenon with most of the global population opening accounts! He had a tremendously powerful vision and changed the way the world communicates forever. We do not all have to change the world. We can just focus on making our life awesome and in turn inspire others to do the same. The more inspired you feel about your vision, the easier it will be for you to magnetise what you need for your own authentic success.

I have walked the path of many of the personal development teachers, from Tony Robbins to Oprah Winfrey, Wayne Dyer, Marianne Williamson and one of my favourites Eckhart Tolle. The latter three authors veer more towards the goals of developing your spiritual side than externally focussed goals. I have incorporated some of the philosophies over the years and now use a heart-centred, authentic style of 'goal setting' that I am sharing with you in this book and continue to develop.

My goal for you is to develop your OWN unique habits of success by being open to your potential future and visualising it clearly (For those of you that may struggle with visualising goals, use a medium that works for you such as writing or audio.) As I am a visual person, this method has worked very well for me. For other clients, we have recorded their dreams on audio or gone into detail in a written/typed format, we have even shot videos! Test it and run with feels good to you. Adapt and change where necessary. We will go into much more depth in the Mind over Matter section. Now back to your END STEP, Your 'Big Picture'.

The title of this chapter, 'Acting the End Step' is all about getting your subconscious and conscious mind focussed on the reality YOU want to CREATE! Remember, every thought you think, every action is energy. So keep focussing on what you do want, keep the energy as positive as possible (we are all human and have other emotions to deal with, but the more consistently you can welcome this positive energy, the more you will 'feel' and 'see' the changes you wish for.

In this section, we are going to look at the 'Big Picture.' We are going to take you forward in time, a bit like Scrooge in a Christmas Carol, to look at your epitaph. We are then going to work backwards to see what actions you need to take TODAY to ensure you do everything you want to in your life, while you can!

Life is Not a Dress Rehearsal

I am sure you have had those moments in your life where you have gone "Wow that was a close call" or someone close to you had a bad experience or worse and you think to yourself, "This life is precious there are some things I need to sort out and do as soon as possible!"

My mother died of cancer at forty-four years old. She used to carry a key ring around with her that said 'Life is not a dress rehearsal' on it. So this phrase always had a special meaning for me. She helped me understand that we have to make each day count. She also instilled in me a sense of humility, a sense of giving and being kind to others. She was a very wise woman and died way before she had a chance to affect the world, as she would have liked. This has given me the impetus to carry on what she wanted to teach me. She was my greatest coach.

Why am I here?

Her death had such a profound effect on me; I was only twenty years old. I started to ask myself deeper questions like 'why am I here?' "What is all this for", "Why did she have to leave so early, now I have to make all my decisions on my own!'

This last question is unlikely to be answered. To ask "Why?" can lead to circular thinking. Instead of thinking "Why?" think "WHAT?" as in, "What can I actually DO ABOUT IT?" This keeps me positive when the not-so-great things in life knock me down. I am sure you may have a similar story or event somewhere in your own life. What did you learn from it? What transpired from the event that was positive now looking back?

Now that I am older, I see that my mother's death brought out a much stronger desire to help people, a desire to make a difference, to make my life and the lives of others count while we are here. I now accept it was part of my journey. That does not stop the days when I am writing and I think of her, and then just start crying, as I miss her very much.

When I got married and gave birth to my baby daughters, I had so many questions I wanted to ask her. I wish she was here for me to ask her the big questions, such as how do instil discipline and courage in my daughters? In addition, ask her the little questions, such as how do I get Ava to brush her teeth without a tantrum and how do I get Rosie to be happy when no one is holding her?

Just thinking about her is enough to get me blue. However, I do not give myself a hard time. I just have a little chat with her, tell her I miss her and I love her and to keep watching over her two granddaughters with love, light and wisdom! My mother used to say, "What doesn't kill you makes you stronger." Humans are amazing beings with the strength to face just about anything. When we put our heart and soul into our desires, particularly with a longing to help others, it does not take long for Providence to reply.

When the Going Gets Tough

On other days when I do not feel like doing anything towards my goals, (yes even positive gurus need some time out!) I remember how lucky I am to be here and what I am supposed to be doing. Every one of us has a purpose, a path to authentic success. Every one of us has our own journey and for the most part, we already HAVE the answers. We just need to be willing to listen and keep an open mind. Listening is one of the challenges of today's information-overloaded lifestyle. So to truly connect with the authentic you, be open to finding and making the time to listen. This is usually a new skill my clients develop when they work with me. They quickly start to see the benefits of their 'quiet time', 'calm session' or 'meditation'. Whatever you like to call it, it creates a way for you to find answers yourself, and for you to 'feel' that you are on track. It is a skill that everyone can learn, even you, if you have not already. All you need is a little guidance, a sprinkling of patience and a dash of faith. There will be more on this later in our 'Mind' Chapter.

Life Challenges are Turning Points

Quite a few of my clients come to me when they are in crisis, it may be post-divorce, empty-nest syndrome or post cancer, or after a lay-off. They are looking for answers; they need clarity and want more from life. Usually there is a discrepancy between what they know and are currently doing, compared to what they could achieve in all areas of their life, particularly financially. When you start excavating what is most important in your life and you create boundaries and clear priorities, the stress starts to dissipate and you win clarity and empowerment.

As I mentioned earlier, some individuals know from birth what they are destined to do. They triumph in life because what they are doing is based on their 'authentic self', using their unique talents and abilities and following their passion. Some of us, like me and perhaps you, take a little longer to figure it out. I have spent quite a substantial amount of time and money on personal development over the last fifteen years in order to get to where I am today.

I have figured out why I am here and what I need to do now, which is to share my experiences and knowledge with you, and people like you, so that you too can perhaps do the same. To feel happy and fulfilled, spending time with people you care about, doing something you enjoy. Otherwise, people can be left wondering 'what is it all for?'

Have you had your Wake-Up Call Yet?

On 9/11, I was in Hawaii, on a course on the Big Island with a legendary American Motivational Speaker. I was sharing with six other girls a gorgeous condominium. I woke up at 7 a.m. and could hear crying from one of the other girls room and I thought to myself "What is going on?" I stuck my head around the door and all the girls were watching the TV. I could see quite clearly a plane going into the side of a huge steel blue skyscraper and vicious flames everywhere. In my head, I thought, "Why are they watching 'Die Hard' at this time in the morning and getting upset over it?"

Then they revealed the news to me about what had just happened in New York. I was speechless! We realised that from that moment on, the world was definitely going to change! It certainly made me sit up and think WHAT and WHO is IMPORTANT in my life? What did I need to change? I called all the people who were special in my life and made a list of things I was going to change and things I should do as soon as I returned home.

The other realisation that struck me, was that I had flown in through New York a couple of days earlier … So it could have been me on that plane! That thought alone was enough to make me feel massive amounts of gratitude for simply 'being alive'. Later in the seminar room, I learned that about 150 of the people were from New York.

One girl had a fight with her boyfriend before she came to Hawaii, because she was unsure if she wanted to get married yet, however, she had a couple of breakthroughs on September 10 and was now clear that she was not scared of commitment any more. She would call her man to tell him so and confirm that they could make their wedding plans when she returned to New York. She tried to call him, but as we were five hours behind New York time in Hawaii, she left a voicemail on his mobile phone.

Her boyfriend worked in the World Trade Centre. He got her message and returned her call, but she was still sleeping when the planes hit! She checked her mobile as soon as she heard the news and the words she relayed to us were "Hi honey, I got your message, that's great news. I am so happy that you have made that decision. I am at work and there has been an explosion and there is fire everywhere. I don't think I'm going to make it … I will love you always."

When she told us all her story, I do not think there was a dry eye in the house. To the best of my knowledge, she went on to start a foundation to help people. She felt she had to do something that was bigger than her. It is an experience that none of us will ever forget.

Action Station

So, after reading that story are you inspired to think bigger? Are there some things you know in your heart you must do? What are they – Write them down now. Some people refer to this as "The Bucket List," as in 'things you will do before you kick the bucket'!

(If you get a chance to watch the movie "The Bucket List," starring Jack Nicholson and Morgan Freeman – you should do it. This film certainly inspires you to do something with your life NOW!)

The next question sounds morbid, I know, but occasionally when you still cannot pinpoint exactly what your big picture is, this technique helps; Remember, you are here on this earth for a reason, 'a purpose', so these questions will help you isolate what that could be, if you do not know or feel it already!

If you only had 1 year to live, what would you do with it?

If you only have 6 months to live who would you spend it with? What would you attempt to do?

If you only had one month to live, what then?

What would you want your eulogy to say?

What would your tombstone say?

These tough questions will assist you to highlight what is MOST IMPORTANT to you and cut through some of the confusion that you might have!

So looking at the above answers, what is or are the key things that you would have wanted to achieve in your lifetime?

Congratulations, you have now completed Chapter 2. Now we need to build on your answers here and start to create a Road Map to Authentic Success by establishing your Goal Path Strategy!

Summary of Chapter 2

- ✓ You now know about creating a vision for yourself that is the 'Final Picture'. You have a better feeling of what makes you happy and why you are doing anything right now!

- ✓ You will have a clearer understanding of 'Why' you want something, as you will have read the touching story of the girl who suffered a deep personal loss after 9/11. You will have a better overview of what is truly important to you.

- ✓ You will have an idea of which mentors or people you most want to be like and can start to 'model'. Observe how they do things and maybe even approach them yourself!

- ✓ You will be feeling extra confident about where you are going and your energy will have shifted to accommodate the process of attracting more of what you want.

- ✓ Visualisation is key to your success and now you can begin to do this regularly. (Remember to claim your bonus mind programme at www.amandasteadman.com/bonuses to help you with this)

- ✓ You are now aware that even if it doesn't go according to plan, it's a learning experience and you naturally take 'another turn' into something new!

Step 3. Goal Path Strategy (GPS)

> *"Be willing to take the first step, no matter how small it is. Concentrate on the fact that you are willing to learn. Absolute miracles will happen."*
>
> **Louise L. Hay.**

Your Flight Coordinates

Pilots set their destinations using high-level instruments within their cockpit. To the everyday passenger, this is nothing unusual. We get in the plane, leave our starting airport, and arrive at the destination airport. We are usually very unaware of any of the problems or technical details of how the plane actually got us there.

I did not know until recently that even though the pilot sets the plane's flight path, it is knocked off course most of the way! The guidance system has to keep tweaking its flight route to ensure it reaches the destination. It is the same with the human being creating their Goal Path Strategy (GPS).

Goal setting is like a compass, or satellite navigation system that you may have in your car that guides you in a particular direction. It is part of your learning. I used to get so frustrated when the outcomes I set DID NOT HAPPEN within the time fame I set. I used to let this thinking and emotional overload hold me back. But NO

LONGER! I now trust that if I set the goal, I want it passionately, I visualise it, I compile a vision-board and written end steps around it, and then I let it go, releasing all emotional attachment to the outcome. I will take the necessary action steps but I will not beat myself up if it does not happen exactly the way I planned. Usually the Universe delivers something I never even imagined that is better than my original idea or desire.

Do not let doubt hold YOU back. Once you get hold of your purpose, your true destiny with your own goals – inspiration moves to assist you. I know I keep repeating this, but I have seen this repeatedly in my life. When all the chips are down, an email or chance meeting occurs with the right answer or opportunity for me to get back on track.

Turning Challenges into Opportunities

A few years ago, I had to let a business go. I had spent quite a few years building it up, but it was not making me happy. I persisted as the money was great but eventually the Universe decided for me and 98% of our clients stopped hiring. We were used to maxing the credit cards (as I used to pay them off in full every month) on expensive holidays, eating out, treating our families and it all stopped within the space of weeks not months! I had huge credit card bills that needed to be cleared and properties that had to be supplemented.

It was a real mess and at the time I did let some negativity settle in before my now husband and I picked ourselves back up and started focussing on the future again. We put in place some plans to pay off the cards fast, moved some savings around to sort the properties out and adjusted our standard of living dramatically for a period of time.

It was in fact a gift from the Universe, although it did not feel like it at the time I can tell you! I had to tune in, to listen and figure out what the next steps were going to be. This was my chance to uncover what authentic success meant to me!

I started to ask a different question. How can I add more value to others? How can I build my client's businesses faster? This is when our business took a different turn and we started afresh. We focussed more on finding solutions for small businesses and our livelihood started to grow again. I was asked to train others on how to do it and to speak at various events. The Universe works in mysterious ways, and sometimes out of ashes, flies the phoenix, even if it takes a little while to realise it!

Do not Worry About being Perfect Just Be Happy!

Since that particular challenge, I kept meeting inspiring writers and getting signposts to do more writing, and I have not looked back since. My life is not 'perfect' but it is wonderful. I write, I am a transformational leader, I change the lives of my clients positively and assist them to break through challenges to find authentic success, I spend time with my two beautiful daughters, I live near a gorgeous beach, and I have a fabulous husband. It feels PHENOMENAL! These were all goals that I set for myself; this is the life I wanted. I am happy, I feel good about myself and I want the same for YOU.

As a coach and mentor, I always believed you have to set the 'perfect' example and do everything 'perfectly', to be an angel to be infallible. In reality, human beings were just not built that way. I thought I would have to have accomplished every one of my goals FIRST, before I was worthy of being listened to, before I could make a difference, before I could write a book, before I could be a mom, before I could be successful. This is not true.

I have found over the years that so many of my clients had the same challenge. They could only be 'successful' or 'start that business', 'be in that relationship' or' finish that book' after all their ducks were lined up, essentially when SOMEONE GAVE THEM PERMISSION. They were waiting for someone to say, "You're okay, you know enough, just do it. Commit!" A coach can officially give you that 'permission,' that nudge, that extra confidence. It helps to have someone who believes in you who is not a close friend, partner, or family member. I want you to know that you can also give yourself whatever permission you need! Authentic success is available to everyone; you just need to reach for it.

Even for me, it took a few friends, colleagues, editors and book coaches for me to consider even releasing this book. I know if this book gets into the hands of at least ONE person and changes their life positively. It was worth it (I am visualising millions of people reading this and look forward to updating this chapter!) So I decided to forgive myself for not being perfect, to give myself permission to just be myself and speak from the heart, to be authentic. If this message does not resonate with you right now, you may not be ready yet. However, that is OK; you know where I am when you want to pick up this chapter or book again. You know when you are ready for your next steps. Providence keeps nudging you and putting different people in your life to guide you, to recommend books (like this one, feel free to pass it on too) or attend a particular course, be prepared to listen and act when necessary.

You are generally only sent the right message or teacher when you are ready to learn the lesson. I trust with all my heart that you, yes you, reading this are willing to believe you deserve more, that you have a purpose here and that these goals and desires you are choosing to pursue now are truly lighting that fire within. Getting that motivation going to make YOUR mark on the world, whether it is being a better mom, friend, business owner, writer or coach is not always easy, but when you know you're going in the right direction it usually feels pretty good! Start trusting in yourself right now and let your journey unfold.

Now you know what is most important to you. How do you know what to work on first? Let us look at the Action Stations for this Chapter.

Action Station – Part 1

Take the list of your goal related answers from your Action Stations in Chapter 1 and Chapter 2 and arrange in a new list. Number them in terms of importance to you and urgency.

Priority 1:

Must Do – these goals must be achieved if you are to consider yourself successful. (Remember you can make the barriers to success as low or high as you want. Baby step goals and actions count too!)

These are your highest priority goals.

Priority 2:

Could Do – In order to consider yourself successful, these goals should be achieved (but it is not essential)

Priority 3:

May Do – self-explanatory!

Once you have your initial list of goals. You can repeat this process for all areas of your life. The most common areas, with examples that are categorized as mentioned in Chapter 1 are:

- **Personal** – I am a transformational author and entrepreneur.
- **Family** – spending time with family, family holidays, I am the greatest mom.
- **Career** – becoming the best sales person, becoming a New York Times Best Selling Author

- **Financial** – I am now earning $15,000 a month through online courses, products and personal mentoring.
- **Physical** – I now weigh 50kgs/110lbs
- **Spiritual** – I meditate twice a day for 40 minutes, I go to church once a week
- **Mental** – I visualise my goals daily; I go to the cinema to relax my head (depending on what film you go and see!)
- **Community & Global** – I donate 10% profits to Sobell House Hospice, Oxford for cancer patients; I devote 2 hours a week mentoring teenage girls.

These may prompt you to cover areas that may have not come up in your initial questioning phase. Below is another technique to enable you to pin point the steps within the goal and how to move forward. If you create goals in a particular format, I have found that these tend to work quite well. I like to call them Your H.E.A.R.T System. HEART is an acronym to break down the goal components:

YOUR H.E.A.R.T. ♥ System

- **H**AVE IN PRESENT TENSE
- **E**XCITING AND ETHICAL
- **A**CTION ORIENTATED
- **R**EASONED
- **T**IME-RELATED

Once you have done this we need to add another layer, to make certain that the goals are structured in a way that they are, not just wants written down with no plan to be fulfilled or how to be measured. Otherwise, they just become unfulfilled desires and dreams! The HEART system will help you do this. I have called it the HEART system as I wish you to remember *that this should not just be a mechanical process* but that you check in with your 'heart' to feel if you are going in the right direction. It is also an easy way to remember how you can format your **'heart's desires'**! Over the next few pages, I have gone into detail about each component and how it has worked for my clients and me. At the end, you will be able to apply this knowledge instantly in the Action Station with the ♥ Goal Sheets. Let us begin with 'H' the first part of the H.E.A.R.T system:

H: HAVE in Present Tense

A goal is a well-defined target that gives you clarity, direction, motivation and focus towards what you desire. Your goal statement needs to reflect this. Your goal statement is a clear written description of exactly what you want. The goal needs to be significant enough to inspire you to move toward the life that you want. Either it will be towards something you want, or away from something you don't want. If your goal statement is vague, you will find it difficult to achieve, as your definition of success in this case will also be hard to define.

From my experience and that of some of the seasoned gurus in goals setting, they recommend putting all your goals into the **present tense**, as if it has already happened! Many of my clients are huge fans of this style used in the example at the end of this

H.E.A.R.T section. We will go into more detail on this in the next chapter and give you more tools how to bring your outcomes to you more easily. Suffice to say that if you repeat and write your wants in the present tense – your subconscious finds it difficult to differentiate between what exists and what needs to be 'created'. So if you keep stating what you want in the present tense (as well as pictures – see Vision Board in Making it Happen) it makes it easier for your subconscious to attract it by placing the right circumstances in front of you.

Results from Using Present Tense and Trusting

As I develop my intuition and goal magnetism techniques, I can see things manifesting more regularly and I have put as much emphasis on teaching you this through goal setting. What I have found, is that you start to believe and trust **more**; your life seems to flow with increased ease. That is not to say you do not have dramas or negative events.

I still get quite a few, but my clients and I also attract many 'surprises' too, like free dinners, empty car parking spaces, the domain name that was needed was available, receiving an unexpected tax rebate, a free weekend away, a discounted course, a hoard of new client referrals without marketing, a new mentor appears from nowhere in an email Inbox, family receive an unexpected gift, you receive an email regarding an expert you needed to connect with, numerous leads for a new project, new tenants for a property via neighbours and she is a cleaner - he is a builder - marvellous.

These are not always massive life goals that we set. At the time, I remember thinking or reading magazines, or passing a restaurant pondering, "Ooh I'd love to eat there" or "I need a car parking space close to the doctors." It may have been a few seconds in my mind, I let it go, forget about it and the items just turn up. How would you like to experience more of this abundance in your life?

Your Own Techniques

What you may find once you get into your own routine of 'outcome setting'. Is that you may not have to write pages and pages of goals, you may not have to do a vision board for every single element of your life. When you get to a certain level of awareness, you can just think about what you imagine may be a great option, make a note in your diary, or cut and paste a picture onto your desktop, forget about it and let Providence decide if it is for your highest good or not. Once you have tried and tested this book's techniques there will be specific ones that feel right and work for you so focus and expand on these.

The next part of the H.E.A.R.T System ♥ is 'E' for Exciting and Ethical:

E: Exciting and Ethical

Exciting goals keep you on track. They fuel the fire of your passion for the goals completion. If you are not excited about your goal, it may not be the right outcome for you! Sometimes, it is tempting to set too many outcomes at first. The problem is, you could "go into overwhelm" and lose your enthusiasm. It can be easy for that initial excitement to fade if your 'WHY' for the goal is not strong enough. Therefore, I suggest that you prioritise your goals. This helps motivate, inspire and test that it is what you really want. Otherwise when action steps and accountability are set, and you don't want to take action because it is not important enough to you, how likely is it you will complete the set tasks? In this case the 'WHY' gives you the leverage to ensure you are moving forwards instead of backwards.

Goals also need to be ethical. By ethical, I mean that they are for the good of all concerned. An example of an unethical goal is, "I want to be rich any way I can (even if it means selling a product you know is not what it says it is, or another poor quality product)."Be honest with yourself and others. In today's Internet age, your reputation can be ruined quickly. Do everything with integrity and from the heart and people are going to recognise that. Your authenticity is what makes you unique. Many people are looking for leaders right now, someone who says what they will do and does what they say. Authentic success will only come if you ARE YOURSELF and stand by what you believe in.

The third part of the H.E.A.R.T equation is based on 'doing something', it needs to be 'Action-orientated:

A: Action-oriented

You will need to develop a strategy for how you are going to achieve your goal. You do not need to know all the details at first, just start with a general plan and key initial action steps. Focus on actions you can take that are in your direct control. It is not necessary to plan every single step as I have mentioned before.

What I have found for clients and I, is that when you set the goal, and you become emotionally involved and passionate about it, suddenly people, situations and opportunities start to appear. You just need to take ACTION on them! The HOW will not always present itself right away, but as long as your heart is in it and you are doing something toward the goal, ideally daily, you will be amazed at what you can accomplish.

When you start taking action, **you cannot manage what you do not measure!** It is easier to track progress against a goal if you can gauge it along the way. Some goals of course are easy to calculate – weight loss, running speed, income. Others are difficult to determine, as there are no apparent quantities that define it such as 'I want to be more confident'; I want to be assertive'. In these cases, you will need to develop some kind of ranking or scale system, or measure time spent on the goal. For example, on a scale of one to ten, ten being super confident, you may rate yourself as feeling only at a level five of confidence. So once you have this rating, you can now set a goal to get to a ten out of ten and then take specific actions you know will increase your level of confidence. Measuring your goals helps you determine if you are going in the right direction and if you need to make any adjustments along the way.

Now that you have three of the system keys, it's important that the goals are in line with who you are and that you do not make them so BIG, that you overwhelm yourself and give up at the get go! So let's look at 'R' the next part in the H.E.A.R.T ♥ System.

R: Reasoned

Goals need to be relevant to you and to your life. They need to be meaningful and significant, in order to make a difference in your life. Remind yourself why you want to achieve this goal. Naturally, when you start out the actions need to be within your control, you can take some baby steps whilst you build up your courage. When working with clients we break each goal down into manageable actions otherwise it is easy to go into overwhelm and feel like the goal is just not 'realistic' or achievable! It is possible to keep the Big Picture in your mind, and focus on each step or action at hand.

For example, I may want to set a goal that I would like to become the next Women's Wimbledon Tennis Championship. It may be a worthwhile goal, but I do not think it is too realistic for me at the tender age of, well let us say over 35 to start training now. Plus, I have great difficulty just seeing where the ball is in order to hit it! All big, scary goals start with the first step, so one-step at a time.

Last but definitely not least is 'T' that represents our time element within the H.E.A.R.T System ♥. Let's see how we can apply this to the goals you are now envisioning.

T: Time-related

"Goals are Dreams with deadlines"

- Diana Schart Hunt

For goals that have a measurable finish ending (e.g. weight loss goal), it is important to set a deadline. Goals without deadlines lend themselves to being put off until another day. We have all said, "I'll start my diet tomorrow." It is easy to put things off isn't it? I did that for quite a while with this book. I kept making excuses, Yes, I have used them all, but I got there in the end and YOU CAN TOO).

What if you miss a deadline?

As a Virgo star sign, I can be quite good at bashing myself over the head because I have not hit goal deadlines. I have learned that 'Time bound' is a great 'guideline' for you. It is not set in stone and should move with you and your life and outcome changes. Everything happens for a reason. If something is not always completed on time, an extra special alternative option is just around the corner for you. When working with clients if they consistently miss deadlines on everything we set together, the goals may not be aligned with who they are and what they really want. Or, they are just not ready to commit to changes in their life at that moment.

Other clients have shifted goals by weeks (especially if weight related), months (if designing a way to leave their corporate career), or years if they are becoming financially independent. In a nutshell, SET a complete date and SET daily/weekly/monthly steps (I discuss scheduling again in the Making it Happen chapter.)

Below is a **written example of goals set within the H.E.A.R.T System** where you can see each part of the formula being used (mentioned in brackets) After the written version, I have inserted a copy of the ♥ Goals Sheet. It is one of the forms that we use in sessions with clients to make it easier to get all the information on paper in one go. Start thinking about what you are going to write as you read these examples through. After this written example, you will find **a table format example of goals in this system** in the second part of the action station.

Note: there are downloadable versions in the bonus resources so go to http://www.amandasteadman.com/bonuses and follow the instructions online in order to have instant access to printable copies.

H.E.A.R.T ♥ Goals System – Short Written Example:

"I am so happy and grateful that it <u>is</u> December 2018. <u>I am</u> the best sales person in the team and <u>reach</u> the £1,750,000 team target [PRESENT TENSE, EXCITING & ETHICAL, TIME-RELATED]. I <u>ensure</u> that I complete 30 sales calls per day that result in at least 12 sales per month [ACTION ORIENTATED, TIME-RELATED AND REASONED]. I am excited about this goal as I <u>prove</u> myself within my new company and with the extra sales commission. I read one book per two months on Sales Experts and talk to the current Top Sales Team leader, which increases my knowledge and skills [ACTION ORIENTATED, TIME-RELATED & REASONED]. I <u>donate</u> 10% of my earnings to UNICEF, which makes me feel good and changes the world for the better [PRESENT TENSE, REASONED & ETHICAL]. I spend every weekend with my family sailing, swimming and dining out. I am now in Disney World with my family for two weeks [PRESENT TENSE, EXCITING AND ETHICAL].

 I am happy, healthy, fulfilled and I am very grateful for everything [PRESENT TENSE, REASONED & ETHICAL]"

Go to www.amandasteadman.com/bonuses for access to a downloadable copy of this short written goal example AND the AUDIO version. They will assist you to complete the rest of the Action Station from this chapter.

Action Station – Part 2

Now take your Prioritised Desires and put them into the HEART SYSTEM. I have created a table on the next page to make it easier for you. Focus on your Top 3 for this action station. Look at the example form and use it to guide you through each of your goals. I find that if most people have more than three BIG goals they can sometimes lose focus. One of my friends Hitesh says, "Focus and timing are everything."

You get what you focus on, so focus on what you WANT - not what you DON'T WANT! Have fun with it, get into a good mood (like play your favourite music in the background), and let your pen (or fingertips on the keypad) go crazy.

Go to: www.amandasteadman.com/bonuses to access a downloadable copy of the H.E.A.R.T Goal Sheet so you can print as many as you need!

Example: My ♥ Goals Sheet:

HEART ♥	Goal:	Write down any action steps to start making it reality
HAVE in PRESENT TENSE	I am now 100lbs/55 kilograms I vibrate with energy and use this to spend more action time with my kids	
Exciting	My reward will be a massage a month if I complete my 3 sessions and at least one new healthy recipe a week.	Put a picture of my head on the body of Charlize Theron and visualise SLIM!
Action Oriented	I will do this with a friend Gym at least x3 a week Work with Personal Trainer to hold me accountable. An accountability buddy to keep me focussed when I want to go and eat CAKE!	Join a gym Re-read the healthy eating guide Get my bike out Call Zoe to train together Put it in the IPod Call Gym today
Reasoned	This is a realistic goal I know I can achieve if I am focussed. It's great for my health and vitality I vibrate with energy and use this to spend more action time with my kids!	Keep writing my ideal weight down
Time Bound	Over the next 12 weeks starting today	Schedule it in PC Calendar and Mobile

Blank Example: My ♥ Goals Sheet:

HEART ♥	Goal:	Write down any action steps to start making it reality
HAVE in PRESENT TENSE		
Exciting		
Action Oriented		
Reasoned		
Time Bound		

Blank Example: My ♥ Goals Sheet:

HEART ♥	Goal:	Write down any action steps to start making it reality
HAVE in PRESENT TENSE		
Exciting		
Action Oriented		
Reasoned		
Time Bound		

Congratulations!

Now you have completed your initial **Goal Path Strategy (GPS)** using the **H.E.A.R.T. ♥ Goals System**. Before you go any further, let us review what you have done so far and if we are on the right track for YOU.

So consider and answer the questions below:

1. What is your current position in relation to this goal?

2. What is your proposed goal measurement system?

3. What resources do you need to achieve this goal and what has to be prioritised?

4. What specific steps are needed to achieve this goal, including estimated time frames and deadlines?

5. What is missing? What are the recurring ideas?

6. Where are the connections between goals? Where can you create maximum leverage and optimise your time?

Once you are happy with what you have written so far, ask yourself:

   1. Am I committed to undertaking the actions I have prepared?

   2. Am I committed to achieving the action items within the timeframe I have set? Is WHY I want it strong enough to inspire me forward?

   3. Am I convinced that this is what I really want?

   4. Am I excited about the outcome from this goal?

   5. Am I prepared to allocate the necessary resources?

   6. Does it FEEL GOOD if I think about achieving this goal?

If you are not answering in the affirmative, with a YES, for all the answers above you need to go back to Chapter 2 and your answers to the earlier action stations in this chapter to establish WHY. Unless you tackle lack of motivation at this particular stage, your heart and mind will not be involved in the outcome and it is unlikely the "goal" will happen. It has to fire up your passion; it has to make you want to get out of bed in the morning.

Naturally, for some of the smaller goals or steps you may not have the same burning passion, but **your MIND and HEART must be convinced** it's what you really want in order for the rest of this book and your list of goals to work for you!

If the answers to the above are resounding YES, then let us move on to Making It Happen!

Summary of Chapter 3

- ✓ You don't have to be perfect, just make a start.

- ✓ Even with setting your goals, they are likely to move and change course as you progress; roll with it!

- ✓ You can break down your goals into categories and start making CLEAR statements about exactly what you want.

- ✓ You can use the HEART system to break down each action step needed. Even if you don't tick ALL the boxes, you have started the process of getting your subconscious mind in sync with your heart and desires.

- ✓ You have clear examples of how to set and write goals by:

    - Having them in Present Tense
    - Being Exciting and Ethical
    - Action focussed
    - Reasoned
    - Time stamped (allow total flexibility here!)

Step 4. I am Making it Happen

> *"Don't wait for your dreams to land in your lap; you've got to get out there and start taking those first steps,"*
>
> - Amanda Steadman

There is a balance between taking action on each of your goals and having a positive expectation that the right people, circumstances and finances will appear. In my experience **once you make a firm DECISION to move in a particular direction, invisible forces you cannot explain move to support you**.

Momentum and good will is created when you apply goal setting. In order to facilitate its progress you DO need to schedule your action steps. So let's look at how you can do this at a practical level.

Scheduling

> *"If you have dreams, acknowledge them, if you want them to be real; schedule them!"*
>
> - Amanda Steadman

This is one of the areas where even the avid goal setter can come unstuck (including myself and clients on numerous occasions) I am particularly good at getting all the goals down on paper, planning resources, getting excited, cutting pictures out, and all the creative side of this process. Then it comes to hard-core planning and scheduling! It did not come easy to me. I have learned to love Excel Spread sheets over the years! However, I know there are more detail-orientated individuals who will find this stage a breeze!

The key to this stage is to **FIND SOMETHING THAT WORKS FOR YOU!** There is new technology every day that can facilitate this process. I am a bit old-fashioned in some ways, as I still do a lot of my goal setting on paper before it goes into spread sheets, pop-ups, and my mobile phone! To me there is something magical when those words go from your brain, through your hand and physically onto that paper. I love doing brainstorming, mind map exercises with clients, and I always get them to **HANDWRITE,** rather than type a minimum of three action steps at the end of our session together. Therefore, the process of achieving the goal has already started! Whatever systems you use to schedule or keep it real for you use it.

Here are some of the examples our clients and we have used in the past:

- **Good old pen and paper**
- **Filofax/Paper Diary**
- **Excel Spread sheet**
- **Laptop/PC/Tablet**
- **Microsoft Outlook/Any PC/Mac Calendar**

- Online Calendars – Yahoo, Google
- Your Personal Assistant/Virtual Assistant
- Mobile Phone/PDA/Smart Phone
- iPod/iPad/iPhone
- Kindle Fire/Tablet
- Alarm
- Goal Card
- Planning Systems
- Journals/Gratitude Books

There are so many Planner Systems available now and it changes daily! Personally, I am now relying more and more on my e-mail, mobile phone and iPod to keep those actions moving as well as a paper diary and journal. If I was forced to choose, I do like to put everything on one piece of paper and tick things off! On top of that, I have a very reliable partner (he's hard core if I am not stepping up!).

I have found through working with clients for many years now, that there is no point in imposing a way of doing the planning. Unless you feel comfortable with it and it fits your lifestyle – you just will not do it! I have seen it repeatedly when we have invented planner after planning tool! So get your goals and steps into manageable chunks and start inserting TIME slots into your preferred scheduler.

If you can do this – and stick to it, you are well on the way to joining the 5% of individuals who set goals and take the steps necessary to Make It Happen!

Some other tips for using the planners include:

- Make sure you add the date to the top of the planner so you always know you are using the current plan. It also helps for future reference.

- Use different colours to indicate your focus for particular blocks of time. Set your own colour scheme for each focus area (for example exercise, family time, time-out, etc.) and use these colours throughout all of the planners you are using, so you can pick out focus areas at a glance. Excel Spread sheets are great for this, I like to make mine visually appealing or should I say 'pretty'!

- Include relevant details for the tasks – What? Where? When? Who? How? This will be most detailed for the daily planners, with decreasing level of detail as the planner outlook increases.

One of the other key ingredients of Making it Happen is having people around you that support what you fully in achieving your authentic goals. We will talk about this in more detail in Chapter Six.

Making it Happen versus Waiting for it to Happen

> *"Sometimes you just have to surrender to your dreams and let the Universe figure out the details."* -Amanda Steadman

There is a balance between 'waiting for' and 'working on' your goals to be achieved. Here is an example in my own life. I wanted to visit the Caribbean so I jotted it down in my diary very briefly 'It is December 2008 and I am so happy that I have now visited the Caribbean.' In my mind, I had envisioned the Sandals couples-only resorts. Their advertising is attractive! I found an advertisement and glued it onto my June of 2008 Vision board and then I FORGOT ABOUT IT. It was on my vision board, which was a picture frame in my bedroom. However, my main goal was to get pregnant so I was not as hung up on the vacation goal. I Let go any expectation and decided to 'wait and see' (still NOT thinking about it)

As it happened by October, I went on a business cruise in the Caribbean (It was a very good deal too) of which I had no idea was available when I did my vision board. Then again, in January 2009 I went on a Marketers Cruise, where I met so many people who propelled me forward in the Internet marketing world. I had not expected either of these trips – nor an opportunity to work in the Caribbean that turned up in 2010. It never fails to amaze me that sometimes the Universe 'over delivers' on your desires.

The events, people and money you are 'supposed' to receive can turn up. Those goals that you THINK are important and may not be for your highest good (like myself, I wanted to win an Oscar in order to move people emotionally, then I get to do that anyway with my training and writing! Are you getting my drift!)?

Some people like spending a lot of time writing their goals up and printing them out and having them on their desktop where they can read them every day. If you are a visual person, then vision boards are most likely the way for you to go. I also have many written goals and goal film scripts (writing out your goals in a story as if it were a movie, as if it was real already – See Section on Detailed Written Goals in Mind Mechanics). Nevertheless, vision boards seem to work very well for me and many other people I know.

Motivation versus Inspiration

Motivation is fantastic, and having a significant amount of it for each goal is necessary. However, I want to mention that when you do get on TRACK, when you are on PURPOSE, you tend to be more inspired and then the motivation comes naturally. If you are finding that you have to motivate yourself and it feels like a drag, you know you are doing something you *should* do, rather than something you *want to*. Then it may not be an important enough outcome, or the right goal for you at that moment.

Yes, there is always some amount of challenge or struggle. However, if you listen to your gut instinct/your intuition you will usually know when you are going down the "wrong" path and can correct yourself. When you are **INSPIRED, MOTIVATED** and

PASSIONATE about what you want to achieve – positive things just start to happen for you and you meet the right people, receive the right opportunities and directions. So get moving!

Let me give you an example of following your gut. I had a business division that focussed on helping female entrepreneurs and I had so many opportunities to work with other leaders in my field, it was overwhelming. I started to work with a business that appeared to be on the same wavelength as me. We were working on particular projects and goals concerning educating and motivating women in business. Within a very short period of time I started to realise that we were not going in the same direction and it just did not 'feel right'. I started to feel uncomfortable with what I was doing. I could not put my finger on it exactly, but something was telling me that even though the project had incredible potential, I was just not destined to complete it. So I pulled back from the venture and felt a great sense of relief. I ended up taking on new projects and found a mastermind group who pushed me and my sense of value forward.

People ask me 'how do you know it's definitely your intuition?' Well intuition has a habit of being very persistent! If you keep ignoring it, it will keep coming back and reminding you that you need to listen! I find I get a sinking feeling in my stomach at the thought of continuing with an action that may not be congruent with my authenticity. This is as close as I can get to a physical signal. I am not always 100% certain whether it is a real 'sign' or not, nevertheless, usually when I have made the 'right' decision. It 'feels' good. I trust this will make sense to you.' Practice makes perfect' with this skill and stay 'open' for feedback!

When it is Not Going According to Plan

> *"I know God will not give me anything I can't handle. I just wish that He didn't trust me so much"*. - Mother Theresa

If you are struggling to make it Happen, it could be procrastination or sabotage that is setting in. Therefore, you need to both revisit the goals and be honest as to how important it is to you at this moment. Not only that, it could be your 'internal warning system' alerting you to a drifting off your given path. Listen out; it could save you much time, effort and heartache. Every challenge can make you stronger.

So with this in mind, let's start making your dreams a reality and start getting your actions in your planner. Set some time aside and Schedule it NOW!

Action Station

Here is your Action Station for this chapter. Follow the instructions below.

1. Schedule Method: Choose your schedule method of choice and start to move all the Goals you have set so far into your system. If you are not sure, just start with the HEART ♥ Goals Sheet and a paper diary or diary linked to your email for example. Keep it super simple until you develop your own style and rhythm.

2. The 'Why': Remind yourself of the reason you set this goal in the first place – your big picture, your motivation, and your focus. Answer examples: I want to spend more time with my children, I want to travel anywhere, or I want to feel good about myself. Keep this in the forefront of your mind to motivate you to continue. Combining your goal actions with your daily habits will help, as it will become "normal" for a goal action to be part of your day-to-day routine.

3. Trust you are on the right path: as mentioned previously, you will get a gut feeling that you are going in the right direction. Otherwise, you may start to be a little stressed and something will be bothering you. You may not be able to put your finger on it, but you will have feeling that it is just not right. If this starts to happen to you, pay attention and revisit where you are, what you are doing and whom you are doing it with!

4. Bite size: Break down daunting goals into more manageable pieces so you can get some action under your belt. For example if you want to earn $100,000/£100,000 per year (or month) break it down into smaller figures such as $8,333/£8,333 per month, $277/£277 per day. Then it does not look as scary. Alternatively, if it is fitness, start by running one mile per day and work upwards as if you are going for a marathon. It sounds simple, but **you can go into overwhelm if you miss this step**. Your conscious mind keeps saying, "You can't achieve that! It's TOO BIG a step!" So **beware of that voice** and ensure your subconscious believes you can. Then, in most cases, it will handle the details!

5. Rewards: Motivate yourself by setting yourself a reward for getting it done -- and an even better reward for getting it done on time. Interestingly, most people feel bad when they procrastinate – that is your subconscious telling you that you are focusing on the wrong things. Your subconscious also rewards you for completing a task by the little "buzz" you get when it is done. In a way, completing a task is its own reward! I am only now remembering to REWARD myself. This also helps to reinforce the success behaviour with the subconscious (great excuse to be kind to yourself and increase your number of treats per month!

Example List of Rewards:

- ✓ beauty treatment
- ✓ going to the football game
- ✓ dinner with partner/friends
- ✓ a beer, glass of wine, chocolate
- ✓ a new car, handbag, gadget
- ✓ your list can be extensive!

As you start to achieve results, motivation to continue will naturally follow. **Use the Bite Size Plan** below to assist you with this.

Take the challenging goal and chunk it down into BITE-SIZE pieces.

Bite Size Plan (BSP)

1st Bite Size Piece I feel comfortable doing right now:

2nd Bite Size Piece I can do:

3rd Bite Size Piece I can put into action:

4th Bite Size Piece action I can do:

Go to www.amandasteadman.com/bonuses for access to a printable version of the Bite Size Plan.

Is there still anything else holding me back or making me feel overwhelmed?

5. Outside Help & Accountability! Enlist the help of a mentor or support group to follow up on your progress.

For Extra Accountability, I invite you to work with me! Drop me note at Amanda@amandasteadman.com

Going the Distance

There are so many tools to help you action your goals. One of those tools is a coach. A coach can give you a fresh perspective, test your passion for each step, and hold you accountable! **Accountability** is a factor that can increase the probability you will complete what you set out to do. Coaches, mentors and mastermind groups are marvellous at this. They like to keep you on track and check that you are holding yourself to a higher level (more on this in the Power Team Section)

Many successful people have coaches and "mentors" that are already successful at what they do. They share their hard-won wisdom, warnings about pitfalls, and secrets of success. Who has already achieved what you want to do? Make a list and approach them directly. A true mentor is usually interested in having mentees. Some mentors accept payments for their services others may not. It depends on who your mentor is and how much time they have! The key here is to not be shy and ASK. The worst that can happen is that they say no! So go for it.

Whenever I have set a goal for a mentor or getting my own coach (yes even mentors and coaches have mentors and coaches!) in most cases they have turned up within a matter of days via friends, associates and the internet! The mentors I had assisted me to progress at a much faster pace, which is what I wanted at the time. Many of the ideas and principles I incorporated into my own life and that of clients. I wanted to use the most updated, results rich strategies! Another time I was looking for great information on transformational writing and publishing and an email to a virtual seminar turned up in my inbox. I do not know where it came from. I definitely did not sign up to their list so even today it is a complete mystery! I got so much of the information I needed plus another mentor within hours of 'putting it out there'.

I am finding that the more you trust, the easier, faster and more accurate the results tend to be. Test it for yourself! You have set numerous goals using the templates above so do note down when it happens. I would love to hear ANY of your success stories so drop me a note; if you like we can put you in the next book! <u>Yes, I would like to share</u> and email me, Amanda@amandasteadman.com.

You already know what you are capable of and with the support of others and the tools described above. You will find the momentum, the energy, and the excitement to make your plans a reality. Extra gentle pressure and accountability go a very long way! It is much harder to put things off and procrastinate if you have told six people that you will definitely finish your book by Christmas or that you will drop a dress size by Valentine's Day! Our clients have progressed massively just through group and individual calls where they have shared what they are going to do with their peers. In addition to this, because they have shared it, the group or mentor is also thinking about their goals and may come across, circumstances, people or information that can assist them to move forward faster.

Staying on Track

Holding my clients accountable is one of my strengths. I have one client who is a wonderful woman. At this moment, she is increasing her confidence and knowledge in her field by getting out there and DOING IT! She has gained a huge amount of practical knowledge and feedback recently. It is great to see that she now trusts her own intuition and can 'sense' that she is now on the 'right path'. She is very intuitive and gifted at listening to people effectively. This week I have held her accountable to getting an audio done to highlight her expertise that she can give away on her website to build her list.

If you have quite large or long-term goals, it is not uncommon to lose a little momentum. This is where the support, encouragement and belief of your 'chosen Power Team' come in handy. I believe most of us want to have a positive outlook at all times, however this is not an easy task and there are going to be days when you want to give up, where you just don't want to put any more effort in. When you feel like this, acknowledge it, bounce your thoughts off someone you know that will reinforce your conviction. Consider the <u>Group Mentoring Programme</u> If you have inkling that it is no longer a goal you want to achieve. Let it go and do not be too hard on yourself for it. Drop me an email at <u>Amanda@amandasteadman.com</u> or check out the details on the website.

Over a period of time, it's likely your 'goal posts' may change and you may feel you want to continue because 'you don't like to fail'. This stubbornness can be good and bad. However if the achievement of the goal is no longer serving you and your vision, be prepared to drop it and take a completely new direction. If you are supposed to reach a certain destination, fate will have a way of still taking you there but you may take a few interesting turns first.

I read a book called 'Feel the Fear and do it Anyway' many years ago. Up until this point, I was petrified of 'getting it wrong' or 'failing'. At the time, I was deciding to change jobs. It was my first job that I was contemplating leaving and going on to my second. I was a little apprehensive of making a change, particularly as I was going from a pure commission based role with lots of potential to a less target driven position. This book made me realise that WHATEVER decision you make it is the RIGHT one, because you will LEARN from it! So do it anyway and if you change your mind, you change your mind and make the necessary adjustments. So what, if any, big decisions are you putting off? Whatever they are, make a commitment to deal with them as you move through these chapters. If you are feeling bold why don't you tackle one right now, today?

Next, we will be looking at how you can use your mind to facilitate the process of getting what you desire even further. Pay attention; this is one of the most important and results-rich parts of going for authentic success and the great thing is – YOU are in the driver's seat!

Summary of Chapter 4

- ✓ Scheduling the action steps in is KEY to making your dreams a reality.

- ✓ Even if you go into overwhelm, there are ways you can deal with it.

- ✓ When in overwhelm and thinking 'I can't do it', choose bite size actions to take and keep moving forward.

- ✓ When the going gets tough, get help! Realizing your dreams may not always be a completely smooth ride! I am here if you need me ;)

- ✓ Sometimes progressing may feel uncomfortable – be easy on yourself and expand that comfort zone as far as you can! It will get easier.

- ✓ Remember to check in with your feelings to differentiate true fear from your inner self telling you, you may be on the wrong road. Listen to the inner voice. Is it inspiration or motivation?

- ✓ **Remember to REWARD yourself** along the way – yes even for the small steps. Your subconscious mind loves goodies!

Step 5. Mind Over Matter

> *"Every achievement, big or small, begins in your mind."*
>
> *- Mary Kay Ash, Cosmetics Magnate*

Mind over matter is one of the most essential parts of getting to authentic success and achieving goals. As we asked you in Chapter Three, "Do you believe and know that these outcomes are really what you want?"

If you study the greats of our time and some of the most successful people in the world today, it is clear that they were driven to succeed. Where did that drive come from? Was it an inner strength in their heart, a voice in their head or a vision in their mind's eye? They just knew they could do it. They could **ALREADY SEE THE END RESULT IN THEIR MIND and for them it FELT LIKE THE RIGHT THING TO DO!**

Mind Mechanics

Mental Rehearsal has been around for decades, particularly with athletes. If you were to interview any sports professionals at the top of their game right now, they would most certainly tell you that mental rehearsal and total belief combined builds their winning mind-set and results in authentic success.

Over the years, I have had the good fortune to spend time with friends and colleagues who are authentically successful in their fields and many of whom are millionaires. I have been able to ask them how they did it. They all say that they envisioned exactly what they wanted, what their company would look like, how they would win over the competition, or how they would build their teams. Even when they had a clear vision, they were not always sure how they would get there. Their journeys were not always easy, they made sacrifices, and their timescales moved. Numerous individuals quoted that "it took me '7' years to be an overnight success!" Despite challenges, they held the picture in their minds, took steps to get there and amazingly, the right money, people, opportunities, and circumstances appeared. They followed the signs, took action, and made mistakes in order to make their dreams a reality. **EVERYTHING STARTED IN THEIR MINDS as well as their hearts.**

This is where we have the advantage over other living things. We can use our imagination and harness the power of this super computer in our head to bring about a new reality. Some refer to this as the 'Law of Attraction', where you use your mind to attract what you want – in its simplest description. Even quantum physicists have stated that there appears to be a Law of Cause and Effect within the Universe and that something can be created from nothing. They also refer to this phenomenon as **'The Field of All Possibilities'** that supports much of what has been said in this book so far. To simplify it even further think of it as energy, the energy and requests are made as thoughts and these eventually become physical. When you start to research the science behind this and how others have used it, it is fascinating with incredible results. This is another discussion not meant for this book! What I *do* know is that what I have shared in this book works and **it can work for you IF you LET IT**.

How to get in the 'Flow'

Quite a few people interpret this 'Law' as sitting in a room and wishing for things to happen. In my experience, it does not quite happen that way! You still require some form of achievement process to get your subconscious and conscious mind focused on your desires. You ignite the **BELIEF** that it has already happened, and you **TRUST** that the money, people, opportunities, and circumstances will present themselves. Then you must make a **DECISION** as to which ones to **ACT** on. So yes, there is effort involved!

What I would like to mention here also is that the **HEART needs to be involved too**. The mind and subconscious are very powerful forces so when the heart gets in on the act too, this is when magic starts to happen. There must be times when you have felt everything was going your way? Everything seems to FLOW so well. You are happy, pleasant surprises and amazing events just 'happen' to you. Listen to your 'gut instinct', your 'conscience'. Do practice tuning in to that positive, loving voice you hear in your head and the answers will start to come. The more you practice these techniques, the more you will begin to experience your own authentic success. The more I use it, the more it becomes a 'feeling', an 'energy' emanating from my heart. Everyone's different, so pay attention to your signs and energy.

Results from letting the 'Attachment' go

I am still amazed when I write a goal down in the morning, focus on it, visualise it, and then let the attachment to it go. I have seen results within minutes or hours, so I know it works – unless all of these hundreds of results have just been coincidence! As I mentioned earlier, even scientists have confirmed that all energy is matter, thoughts create things and if you can harness the power of focus. It is possible to manifest something from nothing. I am keeping it as simple as I can.

For example about three weeks ago I was looking in our lounge space and thinking that if we had a larger unit with more doors on, we can squeeze all Ava's day toys into the bottom cupboards and more of our books and crockery in the places the children can't reach. Then I promptly forgot about it. About four hours later, one of our friends called Per, emailed me to ask if we would like their lounge unit, as they didn't need it in their new place, "would we like to take a look and see if we wanted it?" We popped around and lo and behold, it was exactly what we needed and our friend accepted a bottle of Rose in exchange for it (a good deal we thought!)

Another example is that I wanted to invest in a training course for authors. I noted down the dates in my diary as a goal. I already had money, but I thought very briefly, it would be cool if that just turned up from somewhere else. Once again, I promptly forgot about it. Two days later one of my neighbours, from a property I own, let me know he was installing a heating system. He wanted to know if I wanted to split the cost of the installation. Fabulous – so the money I saved on that transaction was exactly the amount I required to invest in the programme!

What is My Secret?

Countless clients and friends ask me what **'my secret'** is. There is no secret; it is just you and your subconscious mind believing and trusting that your desired result will manifest. Once you get in touch with what authentic success really means to you and believe you deserve it. You start to move in the direction you were intended to a little faster. This is why I named the book, Connect to Authentic Success: 7 Steps to the Destiny you Deserve! I look forward to hearing all about YOUR RESULTS! Do contact me with your stories at Amanda@amandasteadman.com.

You Do Deserve It!

The major block for my clients and I at one point is that we believed we **'DON'T DESERVE IT'**. This is the cruellest trick our subconscious can play on us, as it wants to protect us. Once the subconscious sees you are taking action and you believe the result has already happened (from written goals and other techniques we will cover shortly), over time the mind thinks it's a reality and starts to assist you to get there faster. Have you ever noticed that when you want to buy a particular item, say a car or a plush handbag, you start to notice these items much more? This is your super computer sorting out data, attempting to bring you to a decision or result faster.

L'Oreal's marketing department did their research when they launched the 'Because I'm worth it' campaign. It is a very powerful statement and if used correctly will do more than make your face look fab! **It affirms to your subconscious that you are** indeed worthy and this is the foundation for authentic success.

Whatever your opinion is – test it for yourself.

What other methods can you use to get your mind to produce results for you?

Clients of ours have attracted new business partners, worked with millionaires, taken holidays, and met their gurus, all by using some or all of these methods. **Here are a few more for you to apply.**

Experience the Goal through Visualization

This is one of my favourites, as it does not require extensive writing or research. I can just lie down or strike a Yoga pose and just relax my way to a goal! I focus on my breathing and start to picture a goal from start to finish. Recently this appears to be one of the methods that works best for me, alongside vision boards. You will find your own favourites. In the meantime, test all of these to see what works best for you.

Experience the Goal in Advance through Relaxation &/or Meditation

This method may not be for everyone, especially if you have not yet established a habit of sitting still in silence and emptying your mind yet. Nevertheless, it can enhance goal setting as well your health. Our brains send out so many thoughts during the day plus handling our whole nervous system. It is pretty thankful when you wind down and put your mind into neutral, a calm state. The benefits of this approach are extensive, for my clients, friends and

I; we experience feeling more centred, focussed and calm during the day. It is a new habit to get used to and the optimum time for 'busy' individuals ranges from 15 -20 minutes in the morning and ideally at night. The more you CAN DO, the **MORE YOU BENEFIT!**

This is a skill that I am still working on daily, and it is a little challenging when you have a long To-Do list and two young children. However the more you learn to relax and empty your mind, or at least slow it down for a while. This is when amazing ideas, or answers to questions you may have posed at other times, start to emerge.

Relaxation and Meditation gave me a new paradigm. I have seen the results with clients who at first, could not sit still, then I did guided sessions with them to demonstrate how they could do it for themselves. They find a chink of calm, and leverage it into other parts of their life. Quite a few clients have even recorded their own relaxation audios. Others have bought relaxation music or sounds to help them. I also started that way but now I do not need prompts to get going. It is very natural now. The better I get at it the less stress I experience, the better my intuition gets and the goals materialise with a little less effort.

When I talk to my mentors and listen to interviews with others who are very successful, grounded, genuine and living their life's purpose. I have noticed that they all have some form of meditation ritual. It may be yoga, it may be chanting, it may be listening to soft music, or breathing in silence, there are many methods as there are individuals. My point is, many of the answers you seek are in that personal quiet time, where you face you, where you share space with 'God'. So if you only take one thing from this book right now, at least *take this part and make it part of your daily schedule as soon as possible.* I cannot *emphasize how this alone has shifted my consciousness to a completely higher level.*

You may find you just want to relax or meditate on some occasions and not think of anything! This is fine too. If the relaxation or mediation method sounds like the way YOU want to go, start taking a few minutes every day to just sit in silence, see how you get on and apply the other methods mentioned when you think you are ready for it. Find a way to make that 'space' for you. **It is priceless!**

Experience the Goal in Advance Physically

Have you ever wanted to buy a new car? Well, here is your chance to sit in all the ones you ever wanted! We encourage any clients who have a "car goal" to visit car dealerships and book appointments to test-drive the car of their dreams. Some individuals even put down deposits! The more you immerse yourself in the goal, the more your subconscious is convinced it has already happened or that it should assist in bringing it closer to you.

Take pictures of yourself in the car, videotape the experience, smell the leather, feel the seats. Imagine it is already yours. I used to have a Matchbox BMW on my desk lamp when studying A levels (A qualification taken at College between ages of 16-18 in the UK.) Years later, my partner at the time bought one -- so I got to drive around in a lovely 7 Series Beamer for quite a while!

More examples include visiting the kinds of houses you wish to buy. You can view all the rooms and plan how your furniture would be. If you want to attract an amazing partner - try on a wedding dress or morning suit, if you want to start your own business - work closely with an entrepreneur or a mentor in your relevant field, if you want to be in acting- get onto a film set, be an extra, start doing amateur dramatics. The options are endless – you have NO EXCUSES! So get creative! Please email me with your stories and results. Who knows you could be in the next book!

Written Detailed Goals

Written Goals were mentioned in the H.E.A.R.T ♥ Goal System and in previous chapters. Below is a detailed example of what a 'life script' could be. It talks about a typical day and includes visual and feeling descriptions. The more you can include ALL YOUR SENSES, touch, taste, smell, hearing, seeing, the greater chance there is for your subconscious to accept it as 'done'. The more detail you give it to digest – the better the result! Let us ignite YOUR subconscious now and be inspired by the example below.

Written Detailed Goal Example

"It is now December 2015 and I am sitting in my gorgeous living room overlooking the Pacific Ocean. It is filled with modern but soft furnishings, mostly white with hints of beige. On the walls, I have various colourful pictures and artwork. I have pictures of family, my wonderful, gorgeous, adoring wife, my three beautiful, loving sons and enlightened friends, also the amazing people I have met on my journey. I have pictures of me with Jack Canfield, Oprah Winfrey, Richard Branson, and John Cusack.

My typical day includes spending time with my family in the morning and having breakfast with them, a swim and walk all together. Then I disappear to my 'enlightened' office space to work for a couple of hours, I do my mentoring and mastermind calls via webinar, catch up with essential business items, do an online radio interview, prepare for a TV show interview, whilst my wife entertains the boys!

At lunch Anna our housekeeper prepares lunch and we all sit down together to eat a nutritious and super tasty lunch. Then Anna looks after the boys for 1 – 2 hours whilst my wife and I go through our goals and businesses together, decide on what to delegate to our Personal Assistant Veronica and our IT team. Veronica handles all my travel to and from speaking events all around the world. In the afternoon (not too late) we then leave the 'home office' to take the family to the beach for a while. Then we venture back to our pool to rinse the sand off and head up to the six bed-roomed, detached beach house. We have an open plan kitchen diner that is light and spacious. The whole feel of the house is of light, space, openness and, great energy. The windows all have amazing views especially at the back where you can see over the ocean. It is an awesome space and makes us all feel happy, secure and comfortable.

We are super proud of what we have achieved and love to share it with friends, family and clients. Anna serves our dinner again today, although my wife does enjoy doing the cooking a few times during the week; it gives us extra time with the family and to focus on other items. All areas of the children's creativity and their natural talents are encouraged. They are happy, healthy balanced kids.

Incomes from our businesses bring in approximately £15-25,000 ($20-30,000) a month net, with approximately 3 hours a day management. I love what I do, especially teaching and group mentoring so I do not really class this as work. My clients love what I assist them to achieve and I watch them as they become even greater people and make their positive mark on the world. I am proud to assist them on their journey and inspire millions of others to do the same.

Go to www.amandasteadman.com/bonuses to download a copy of the written goal above to work on.

I am sure you are starting to get ideas on what you could write for yours. I love hearing about what yours are and getting copies of what you have written. Just by getting it down and SHARING it, you are making it more likely for it to happen, so do send me a copy via email to me: Amanda@amandasteadman.com

Goal Cards

A credit card size card with the goal written on it and stored somewhere you look every day, ideally in your wallet or purse. Below are a completed example and a blank version for you to write your own in.

It is December 2015 and I am so happy, healthy, wealthy and grateful now that I am living in my dream beach home and have 2 healthy, happy children and a loving superwoman wife. I have a wonderful inspiring, loving family and friends. I travel internationally 1st Class and 5* hotels paid for by clients (who I add tremendous value to) I earn $100,000 per month net.

YOUR GOAL CARD

Go to www.amandasteadman.com/bonuses to download blank copies of the goal cards to work on.

A Vision Board

What is a Vision Board? Essentially, it is a piece of paper or board and is a VISUAL representation of your goals. We normally recommend having the "End Goals" in pictures. For example, if you want to get married, take a picture of you and your partner in wedding outfits and stick it on your board! (If you happen to be an actor, you will love that one. Even if you are not it does not cost anything to go to a bridal shop and try a few dresses on. I did this in 2009, I already had my man, but it took a while to convince me to go down the aisle. I bought the dress I tried on one year later in 2010, it was my dream dress. Unfortunately I did not get to wear this particular dream dress as by the time it arrived, I discovered I was pregnant and had to order another dress!

Alternatively, you can find another wedding picture and superimpose your heads on top. That is always highly amusing! We have done this with many of clients and friends over the years and its phenomenal how this works for the majority of people. This can be applied to goals and wishes such as getting pregnant to finding the right partner or fortune. I did a superimposed wedding photo with one of my vision boards, my husband-to-be was wearing a kilt and there was a beach in the background. We did get the beach but my husband is French so no kilt this time!

Go to www.amandasteadman.com/bonuses to access **a vision board example**.

If you want to become well known within your field and be interviewed by a big magazine, you can create a cover with YOU on it. You can go to http://www.magmypic.com/magazines where you can make one free! I love all this creative part! Have fun with it. Include your nearest and dearest or your favourite gurus and stars in the pictures. The vision board technique works very well – especially if you are a visually stimulated person!

You can do a picture of you holding a bank cheque for various amounts, or standing next to a pile of money. I have found that doing a photocopy of your bank statement with higher amounts in works quite well.

I tend to use pictures of the LIFESTYLE I want to live NOT JUST piles of money pictures. The end steps of gorgeous villas, boats, holidays and pictures of happy families spending time together mean more to me than the visuals of cash so I have focussed on that. Test it and see what works best for you. Your heart has to be in it, you have to feel the outcome and that it is what you really want. The more authentic if feels to you, the more likely you are to receive it.

Go to www.amandasteadman.com/bonuses to access an example of one of my favourite boards that I did back in August 2009.

There is a picture of a beach wedding – we had a beach wedding similar to the picture. There is also a restaurant top left that resembles a restaurant that we tried for our rehearsal dinner. This board was divided into three parts, my side, my partners and our joint goals. You can do a vision board of ANY AREA you like. I find that for me, working from the centre outwards works well for us! Play!

Here are just a few of the **amazing results** that have come with using **vision boards:**

One of my friends put a picture of a guy she liked the look of in a wedding picture and placed it on the wall in her bedroom. Two years after she started dating a guy who looked just like him!

A client cut out pictures of houses she wanted; they all had to have lovely gardens. After twelve months, she found a house that resembled two of the houses on her board and it had a huge garden. She even got a dog that went with the garden too!

Another client put pictures of clothes and ladies who were two sizes down from her dress size. Within six months she had dropped to almost that size and received a promotion, so she had the extra money to buy the clothes she wanted. She did eventually reach the dress size she wanted but did not feel comfortable with it. Therefore, she decided to be happy at the next size up and still eat most of the food she wanted without being on a 'healthy eating regime' all the time. This is a fantastic example of moving a goal post if it does meet your needs.
Authentic Success has to '**FEEL RIGHT FOR YOU!**'

Another client put a screen saver of an Audi TT and after hitting sales targets well for about 11 months; he finally went out and bought a yellow one! Just because one of your goals is a more 'materialistic' goal, it does not mean it is not authentic. We are here to do things that make us happy and to spread the happiness and success we experience onto others! Part of me believed for a long time that to be successful and rich you have to be cutthroat in business. Due to meeting many authentically successful individuals in business the last two years, I now know that this is not the case! My old paradigms and beliefs have changed into much more positive ones regarding business and money. If you are true to who you are, you will ATTRACT the right clients who NEED to work with you and an income to match that which you GIVE and how much VALUE you ADD.

Even if you are a little sceptical, give it a go. The more you just believe that something 'good' will come out of a situation or decision, the more likely it or something even better is to appear.

Write a large bank cheque to yourself, your family or a charity.

I have used this technique and it works quite well. I have not had a million dollars drop through the letterbox in one go yet – nonetheless I have received new business and random cheques from all around the world. I even received a letter from my grandfather's estate (executed over 18 years earlier), stating that there was an excess of funds in the account and here was the balance! After experiencing recession in our company and making some unfortunate real estate decisions, we needed to find alternative cash flow an in order to pay off credit cards. I wrote down the amount that we needed a month to catch up a little. We received a letter in the post stating that our mortgage company's rates were lowered to £0.11 ($0.17) a month for quite a few months which helped us nicely on our way and enabled us to invest in a new business.

Create a bank account statement with your desired amount sitting in it.

Just simply take one of your paper bank statements, use office whitener to blank out the amount and enter your own! Stick it on your vision board and have multiple copies around work and home. I have experienced refunds and entries that I never expected. DO tell us what you experience! We would love to know.

Screensavers

Have a picture or pictures of your top goals on your computer at home and work, on your tablet, mobile, simply any of your gadgets! Back in 1999 I used to have a screensaver of a Silver Volkswagen Golf Mark 4, SE 1.6 five door (Yes I was that specific) In September 2000 I went to Holland and bought it cash. It was an awesome feeling to drive it off the parking lot and back to the UK! I am still driving her (we have been through a lot together!), says a lot about Volkswagen as a brand doesn't it! Ooh, I could approach VW to sponsor this book!

Record your goals in audio and video

Most people have an iPod, PC, or laptop with some kind of recorder for audio or video files. Video is now available on cameras and cell phones; so it is much easier now to record your own material, in your own way, and make it work for you! How about creating your **OWN AUTHENTIC SUCCESS AUDIO LIBRARY?** This method is very powerful. It does take a little time to compile but once you get the hang of it you can repeat the whole process. There are two free pieces of software you can use for this. For free audio software for your PC or Mac (you will need an in-built or external microphone for the software to work.) Audacity is one programme we use go to http://audacity.com

For free video software (up to 5 minutes of recording time) go to http://jingproject.com – you can upgrade on either for more services but it will get you started. Have fun!

Create a Future Photo Album

Similar to a Vision Board, a future photo album is an album that shows the story of your future primarily in pictures. When you glance through the album, it is as if it has already happened and you are appreciating all the fond memories of all the events and achievements you have realised. So if you wish you could add a made up wedding certificate, birth certificate or anniversary invites. Practically anything that makes it more real.

You can do this as a physical album or set up a folder in your computer or IT gadget and use the slideshow function to view. There are numerous free online programmes to create photo albums, so use your internet browser to find one.

Action Station

Look at your top 5 goals. Take some time out and go to a quiet place (or put your iPod on with relaxing music – whatever works for YOU!) and start to visualise each goal in detail. If you struggle with the imagination part, WRITE OUT each goal in detail, but use all the senses – touch, taste, smell, sight, and hearing.

My Top 5 Goals are:

1.

2.

3.

4.

5.

There is a technique that incorporates some elements from Neuro Linguistic Programming (NLP), which can facilitate and speed up results. I could write another book on this process alone, so suffice to say here that if you wish to know more, drop us an email or visit the site.

Alternatively – use ANY or ALL of the methods described above to ignite your mind to action! Your mind wants to work for you; **the universe is there to support you. You just need to ASK! Maybe start with 3 techniques and test them for effectiveness.**

Important Note:

Frequency of Immersion

Everyone is different. I cannot emphasize the POWER of some of these techniques and how they have worked for thousands of people!

The more you immerse your subconscious into the images, sounds, smells of your END STEP, the more likely it is to manifest and the easier it will be for you. Even if you can only squeeze in 10 minutes a day DO IT. If you add the power of meditation before or during any of these techniques – you are onto a winner! Remember to trust that the result will come (and not always in the time frame you set!) and release the attachment to it.

So now, you have your Goal Path Strategy, The Plan, and The Mind Methods. Now we need to move on to another key part of the puzzle that will keep you on Target and in Tune – Your Power Team!

Summary of Chapter 5

- ✓ Everything starts in your mind. Thoughts create things, so construct those thoughts carefully. You get what you focus on.

- ✓ The law of cause and effect is working **at all times so use it your advantage.**

- ✓ One of the biggest secrets is that, whatever you 'wish' for, **VISUALIZE it with your mind, FEEL it in your heart, then let the 'attachment'(expectation) to the outcome go**.

- ✓ The other biggest secret is to have **absolute 'belief'** that you will get it. It is like an acceptance this it will 'be' – without attachment.

- ✓ Let go of the greatest block to human potential, the belief that 'I don't deserve it'. Replace with **'YES I DESERVE IT'! Repeat frequently ;)**

- ✓ Use all the mind tools at your disposal and hone in on the ones that work best for you; they are priceless if you follow them.

- ✓ The more involved you are with these realization processes, the more likely you are to succeed. Have fun with them.

- ✓ Do them as regularly as you can!

Step 6. Your Power Team

"Surround yourself with only people who are going to hold you to a higher level."

- Amanda Steadman

"**My power team?**" Yes, in order to reach your goals, you will need a team of keen motivators to support you and keep you on track particularly when the path is not running as smoothly as you would like! It is so much harder to do this on your own. One of the major lessons I have learned is that we all need assistance to make progress. Accept the help when it is offered! A power team will **catapult you to authentic success** much sooner. Plus they know who you are, how you tick and may sometimes see before you do, what you must do for your highest good.

If you have a mentor, a coach or a mastermind group holding you accountable regularly. You cannot keep on with the excuses. You must get stuff done. Even I, no matter how motivated I am, sometimes you need that support to back you up when you are dealing with the obstacles that life will inevitably throw you; **overwhelm** being a prime one for the majority of my clients. You need your back up team and positive advocates to ensure you hit your targets and stay authentic to yourself and your values.

For example, if you're supposed to be getting your website done as one of your actions, your coach can asked for an example of the copy you are going to use, what headers and what calls to action you will have on your first page to make sure you capture interested persons email addresses.

If you are starting a book, it is great to bounce the ideas off someone who has already done it, someone who can show you the way, and give you great pointers to make your work better, to reach the best audience, to make your message clear. You cannot do this on your own. You need an editor at the very least! I had a wonderful team of mentors, techies and editors for this book; otherwise it would probably still be on my computer. I found people who had already achieved authentic success in THEIR own field before I enlisted them.

All experts have an expert above them coaching or mentoring them to success. No one in the world today succeeds on his or her own. Get used to asking for and giving help. It makes the process more fun and fast! It took me a while to learn this, as I have always been an independent and resourceful woman. Somewhere in my brain, asking for assistance was interpreted as weak. Now I realise that it actually means you are smart and that you want to get there faster by leveraging the knowledge, time and effort of others.

What is a Power Team?

Your **Power Team** will vary depending on your goals. If you wanted to become a bestselling author, your team could consist of:

- **Your co-author** writing with you
- **Your business partner** – bouncing ideas off each other
- **Your book agent** – getting the best deals and industry networking for you
- **Your publishing team** – adding value to your book process and marketing campaign
- **Your bank manager** – Lending you the finances to get your book published (Unless you are going digital publishing)
- **Your Book Coach/Mentor** – an expert in their field that knows the right shortcuts to take and reduces the time you need to get your book to succeed.
- **Your author peer group** – meet at networking events, online groups
- **Your mastermind group** – a group of people that provide resources, contacts and feedback. Your group should be motivated, understanding, and supportive of you and your goals.

As with a mentor or coach, you can choose your group relative to your goals, for example, one group may be focussed on entrepreneurship; one may be focussed purely on getting a book written. I tested a few until I found two groups that had the same values, drive and experience I needed to move the group forward and myself. The dynamics of the Mastermind Group adds a **magical element** that seems to **speed up the goal achieving process** – if you all are on the same page! So choose your group members carefully. A coach and a Mastermind Group increase your accountability and add energy to support you, in addition, you get to support others, and you pay it forward! Even when the chips are down, your group helps put you back on track.

Conversely, if you have not achieved what you promised you would, they have your permission to be tough with you, too. I was creating websites to sell physical DVD's and I struggled so much with the technology of how to do that. I got so frustrated I almost gave up. My mastermind group held me accountable but also got to the bottom of the fact that I did not want to sell someone else's DVD's. I wanted to sell my own courses and products, but did not have the courage to step up.

So I got a banner done with my new logo, I designed the Success Mastermind Course and started selling it at speaking engagements in UK and Europe. It worked much better than focussing on an area I was just not passionate about. Now I have various courses and personal mentoring that focus on connecting clients to their authentic success – both personally and in business.

Is there anywhere in your life where this is happening to you right now? Can you see where you may need to change your strategy a little? For example, are you attempting to make money in an area that you don't LOVE?

In one mastermind group I joined, almost all of us hit all our annual goals! In addition, they were big scary ones, too! One lady wrote her notice to a job and went off to work for a multi-millionaire, another guy visualised working on an island with gorgeous views, and he went off to Indonesia. One other group member wanted to be part of the faculty of an online training phenomenon. Within weeks she met someone who introduced her to the right person to make it happen! I achieved many of mine, but the most important outcome for me at the time was to get pregnant! And I succeeded with a bit of help from my husband! So if you want to make this process work faster for you -

join a group as soon as possible, to get that needed 'magic momentum'.

Resistance

Regarding my own clients within a business mastermind group and being tough, I had a client who wanted to start a business and leave her job. She planned to do it over an eighteen-month period. She kept doing the research, had the business loan arranged, but could just not bring herself to hand her notice in. Therefore, we had a robust conversation about what she really wanted.

As we went deeper into her situation, it unfolded that she was actually a little happier in her role because her boss had changed and was not feeling as passionate about her business idea nor the franchise she was considering. Her goals had changed. She decided after much deliberating that she would stay where she was, but would be open to other business opportunities. When the 'right' one for her presented itself, she would act on it. She has not found the right opportunity yet and that is OK as she is happy in this new version of her role and is saving enough cash on the side for when it does happen. The rest of the group also supported her in her new decision.

If goal setting and personal development are new to you it is likely you are going to experience some resistance from those that are close to you. Countless clients have witnessed a partner or family criticising them and laughing at their ideas. The bigger your goals, the more intimidating it can be for others who do not have any or prefer a different way of living. Everyone is on their own path, so be prepared to stand your ground on outcomes that are super important to you. When you start on this journey, all sorts of changes start to take place – from your relationships to the possibilities you start to see.

Someone said to me recently **'Stand alone until those who are ready to stand with you arrive.'** One interpretation of this would be that, on occasions you may need to take some time out to figure out where you are going and along the way it may change the kind of people you hang out with – so don't be afraid of that. If you want to make something of your life, the path is not always going to be easy and you need to be prepared to let go of relationships that do not support you in order to make way for new ones to arrive.

The other interpretation that is becoming clearer to me is that, the more I use the tools in this book, the more I realise that once you are standing in your own truth, your own authenticity, the RIGHT PEOPLE will start to FIND YOU and before you know it, you have an amazing group of peers STANDING WITH YOU!

A new client I had last month was new to goal setting. Nevertheless, she soon started seeing herself differently. Now she knows that she does not need to be afraid of thinking BIG and going for what she really wants in life. Despite all her previous conditioning, particularly from her father, boyfriends and bosses she's broken through her old limiting belief that *'I'm not worthy'* to being grateful and accepting her newfound confidence! She has made her wish list for a new desired job and a soul mate. **She deserves it! So why shouldn't you?**

Action Station

So now it is time to start thinking about who you can take on your journey. Below is an example of a **POWER TEAM CHART.** Think about your Top 5 Goals. **Who could be in YOUR Power Team for each goal?**

Example Power Team Chart:

Goals	Power Team Members			
Goal 1: Write a successful Book	Success Coach or Book Mentor	Book Mentoring or Mastermind Group	Publisher	Successful Author
Goal 2: Start a Business	Business Coach	Marketing Specialist	Success Mentoring Programme	Business Partner
Goal 3: Investing in property	Wealth or Property Coach	Success Mentoring Programme	Bank/Alternative Lenders	Real Estate Agents
Goal 4: Lose Weight	Personal Trainer	Gym buddy	Nutritionist	
Goal 5: Grow my business	Business Coach	Internet Marketing Specialist	Success Mentoring Programme	Joint Venture Partners

My Key Power Team People

Who else needs to be in your Power Team?

A Coach:

A Mentor:

A Mastermind Group:

A Membership Group:

Download a copy of the Power Team Chart from www.amandasteadman.com/bonuses

Almost there!

Now you have completed the Power Team section of the book, **your Authentic Success Process** in this book is almost complete. Just one more section to go!

Summary of Chapter 6

- ✓ Surround yourself with only people who will lift you to a higher level and support you.

- ✓ All truly authentically successful individuals have become good at focusing on what they are best at. They realize that delegation is essential for success and that life is a 'team' sport.

- ✓ By being with a 'team' or mentoring group, you create an unparalleled energy that moves you forward much faster than you ever could do on your own.

- ✓ Six degrees of separation – means that in a mastermind group or team, you could only be six steps/people/companies/products/opportunities away from your biggest goal ever!

- ✓ When you have a mentor or group supporting you, getting through challenges becomes a whole lot easier.

- ✓ With a power team, it is harder to use excuses. They will hold you accountable. You have to deliver what you say you are going to deliver, which brings authentic success faster to you!

Step 7. On Purpose

> *"The Art of Purpose is to do what makes us genuinely HAPPY, so we can pass it on and light the passion in others!"*
>
> – Amanda Steadman

'Your Desires drive your Destiny, Purpose provides the Passion!' As you have made your way through this book, you have answered many questions, taken yourself into 'quiet time'; you're harnessing the power of your mind and heart to manifest your desires. With every step you are getting closer to your AUTHENTIC SUCCESS. As human beings, we have layers of conditioning, self-doubt and emotions we cannot always control nor explain. However, our ally is our intuition, our sixth sense, our inner voice that guides us back to the path we are supposed to be on.

As mentioned earlier in the book, the more you listen, the more answers you will get. Your unique talents and abilities will also be clues as to what you are meant to do here in your lifetime. It will FEEL GOOD to do it, it will be the path to least resistance, it will be a way you can ADD VALUE to people that makes you happy, that makes those around you happy, and ideally fills your heart with joy. I LOVE writing and I LOVE getting my thoughts on to paper and online. It makes me smile to know that I am connecting with people, inspiring them to shine 'their light' so that others can follow their example. I am following all my mentors and teachers examples, by standing up and being counted, by sharing my experiences, my 'secrets' with you the reader, my family, friends and clients so this world can be a better place!

Being on Purpose is like being in First Class

Everyone has a purpose it just takes time sometimes to realise it. As I mentioned earlier in this book, some individuals are born knowing it. For some of us including myself it's been a longer journey. Being on purpose is like someone just bumped you to first class. Economy is great, you still get a good meal, good customer service but you can get stuck in the back there whilst everyone else gets off before you and your luggage can get lost! In First Class it is almost effortless. You get speedy check-in, a large comfortable seat with amazing legroom, extra special customer service; everything is seamless from your welcome to your proper glass of champagne and cutlery (that doesn't break!). It feels phenomenal as you stretch out your legs; you take a deep breath and enjoy the ride with all the other lovely people in Virgin Atlantic First Class! As you deserve it!

Here is the Formula:

♥

YOUR AUTHENTIC SELF + SHARING YOUR UNIQUE GIFTS + TALENTS (YOUR PURPOSE)

= ABUNDANCE + LOVE & FULFILMENT

= AUTHENTIC SUCCESS

♥

This is what I wish for you. You have completed almost all the steps so you are well on your way to **Authentic First Class**! There is still a little more to ponder and get your mind and heart working on so let's hone in how you can get clearer on you purpose right now by answering the key questions in the **'Purpose' Action Station.**

Action Station

Here are some key questions for you to uncover what your true purpose is. Even if you do not feel you have all the answers immediately your subconscious will be working on it for you. So note down ideas, feelings that manifest after this exercise!

1. What did you love to do in the past/as a child?

2. What are you naturally good at?

3. What would you do every day even if you didn't get paid for it?

4. What do you spend most of your money on after living expenses, for example – diving gear, fashion magazines, art supplies, books etc. (excluding things like rent, car!)

5. What sparks the creative and passionate you?

6. What do you believe in, what do you stand for?

7. What do people typically ask you for help with/in?

8. What would you do if you knew you could not fail?

These may be some of the most important questions you ask yourself, so take time to contemplate them and get them down on paper. You may be surprised where this will lead you and the clarity you get on exactly why you are here and what you are supposed to be doing!

Remember this is just the beginning of your self-discovery, be patient with yourself and be totally open to doing things you may never have imagined. Listen to that inner voice; it only wants to get you to your destiny faster!

Thank you for investing your time in yourself and this book. I am so excited for you and look
forward to hearing about YOUR next chapter. Talking of chapter I have included **a bonus one** for you, read on!

Summary of Chapter 7

- ✓ When you are happy and on 'purpose' you can inspire others to do the same. Raise the + vibe!

- ✓ Finding your purpose is a crucial quest that your heart and soul are determined for you to uncover and act on.

- ✓ Once you are aligned with your 'purpose', the world is your oyster; it is like being in First Class.

- ✓ Having answered the vital questions in this action station you will now have a good idea of what your purpose is. Sometimes it is shy, so you have to give it time and focus, so it can emerge. Take time out to go within and ASK if it is not clear to you.

- ✓ Pay close attention to the signs Infinite Intelligence may send you regarding being guided to your purpose. They show up in all sorts of ways – people, opportunities and gift. **Once you start asking these sorts of questions – you are going to get the answers, so LISTEN UP!** This is one of the most important parts of finding the Destiny you Deserve!

Step 8. Love the Chocolate Effect – Bonus Chapter!

> *"Once you start to experience the true power of your own mind and how you can manifest your desires – your life takes on a delicious dimension"*
>
> *- Amanda Steadman*

Goal setting for authentic success is a life-long process. For me it has become the 'Chocolate Effect', I started biting off a couple of pieces and then I progressed to eating the whole bar! (For those of you on healthy eating regimes, 70-90% pure cocoa chocolate bars are allegedly **GOOD FOR YOU OK!**) Once I comprehended the power of how this information can transform you, I was hooked! Authentic Success has come through a process of trial and error, challenges, triumphs and gratitude. Persistence and repetition have been skills I acquired and did not come easily!

To me the real key to AUTHENTIC SUCCESS is living a life that makes us FEEL FANTASTIC. I started setting small achievable goals that **made me feel good**. I built on that and kept going, I kept repeating the process, another little piece, another section and yay – I've completed the whole bar, I reach most of the goals I set and it's a fantastic feeling!

Many of my clients are women and had no problem in rewarding themselves with tiny or large pieces of chocolate as they progressed through their goal plans. I remember buying a client a

Terry's Chocolate Orange, (orange shaped chocolate candy in segments that is made with orange oil, are you getting hungry yet?) as she was struggling to get the confidence to sell her jewellery, getting the site sorted and marketing. Every time she completed one-step – she decided that she could reward herself. Amazingly enough she made great progress after that and then switched to other non-chocolate related rewards like, pedicures, long baths with essential oils and a new bag!

I would love to say to you that AUTHENTIC SUCCESS means you will not have any more challenges, that there will not be days when you feel overwhelmed, but that would not be so accurate. What I have learned is that each of the challenges presented are lessons and it is the way that we approach them and our emotions that leads to our inner success and our feelings of fulfilment.

If you are in alignment with what you know feels right and great to you, the challenges become easier to overcome. Your outlook is different, as you will be focussing on what is RIGHT with a situation and not what is WRONG with it. As I mentioned before, you get what you focus on, so when you are being true to you, when you are sharing your dreams and goals with others, when you are comfortable being you and not care what others think about you, you will experience a freedom and a contentedness that you may not have experienced before.

As you review your goals regularly, never be afraid to let one's go that do not fit, and remember to acknowledge what you DID DO and do not mooch on those 'learning experiences'!

What I love about 'The Chocolate Effect' is that it feels great. As human beings, we are motivated by pain and pleasure. You would not have come this far in the book if it did not make you feel more positive. As my mum said earlier in this book, **'LIFE IS NOT A DRESS REHEARSAL'** so make the moments count, figure out a way to do a job that you LOVE and spend as much time with the people that you LOVE. This is your opportunity to wake up to the amazing human being you are with your own unique gifts, talents and abilities. I wanted to inspire you to explore and decide what you are going to spend your valuable life with **PURPOSE** and by remembering The Chocolate Effect! Let me invite you to commit to yourself today that you are going to take action.

NOW is the time to make your decision, NOW is the time you live your life, not tomorrow, not yesterday but TODAY. Stop making excuses, take that leap of faith and TRUST that your DESTINY, YOUR AUTHENTIC SUCCESS will reveal itself.

I trust that this book has served its purpose and I have served mine by igniting the passion, the belief that you deserve a fantastic life because YOU ARE YOU and for no other reason. You just have to be yourself, listen to the inner you and GO FOR IT. I can be with you every step of the way and I invite you to let me assist you on your journey. Go to www.amandasteadman.com to find out more. To get started right away is an Authentic Success agreement on the next page. Now is the time to begin...

Action Station

Authentic Success Agreement

> **Authentic Success Agreement**
>
> I (Your name)_____ declare that I am amazing and have unique gifts and talents that I use to add value to others.
>
> I take action daily and trust my intuition to guide me. I commit to My Authentic Success by being myself and fulfilling my potential completely. I love who I am, what I do and what I stand for - I ROCK!
>
> Your Name:_____
>
> Signed (Your Name)_____
>
> Date_____/_____
>
>
> **Amanda Steadman – Your Witness :)**
>
> Signed (Your Name)_____
>
> Date_____
>
> ;) ♥

Go to www.amandasteadman.com/bonuses to download your printable version.

Congratulations!

Wahoo!

You Did It!

You are AWESOME!

You are BRILLIANT!

Summary

> *"The Secret of Success is being your authentic free self, living in the moment and choosing love and happiness as a daily attitude!"*
>
> *– Amanda Steadman*

What have you learned from this book? Here are some of the results you will have once completing the action stations and finishing this book

- ✓ I have guided you through assessing what is most important to you and turned them into specific goals.

- ✓ You now have clarity and conviction of purpose.

- ✓ You will now have a vision, a clear direction of where you are headed and the signposts and markers that let you know you are on track; including specific tools to ensure you get it done and make it happen.

- ✓ You have started to use your powerful mind to program yourself for authentic success and to let providence know you are ready to receive what you have envisioned.

- ✓ You are allowing your heart (and intuition) to direct you on many of your decisions and you check in with yourself to ensure you are on track as it will feel 'right'!

- ✓ You also have clarity on how to put your dream team together to maximise your success and realise your potential.

- ✓ You have all the steps tools, questions, action stations and inspiring stories necessary to succeed!

- ✓ You have a bonus Mind Programme so you can relax your way to authentic success!

- ✓ You have further free resources to use and apply.

- ✓ You have an invitation from me.

My wish is for you to thrive more than you could have dreamed, I trust I have moved you to take those first, sometimes scary steps forward and **KNOW you are WORTH IT, that you DESERVE IT.**

I would love to continue this journey with you in our programmes, SO DO REMEMBER TO CLAIM YOUR BONUSES RESOURCES - go to www.amandasteadman.com/bonuses

If you have done already and if you would like to work with me personally drop me a note at Amanda@amandasteadman.com

Some more tips before you go:

- Do not worry about making everything perfect. JUST START!

- If at first you do not succeed, go again! Feedback is the breakfast of Champions. There are no "failures" only "lessons."

- Know yourself. Keep focused on YOUR definition of Authentic Success and what is meaningful to you. The "Why" is more important than the "How." …The "How" usually takes care of itself!

- Use all your senses to activate your authenticity and bring those goals closer and faster!

- Keep sight of the "Big Picture," but don't be afraid to shift the goal posts if you have to. Adjustments happen!

- Enjoy the journey

- BE HAPPY & LIVE IN THE MOMENT!

Let me leave with you a parting thought and an invitation →

"Don't leave this world with your song unsung, get out there and be YOU!"

- Amanda Steadman

WHAT ARE YOUR NEXT STEPS TO SUCCESS & HAPPINESS?
Invitation to Work with Amanda

I am grateful and blessed to be able to create systems and opportunities for others globally to "wake up" and to do what they really love, to be successful in life, I get to travel the world speaking, writing, and motivating others to achieve their dreams. As well as doing it virtually online. It is more rewarding than words can say!

If you follow the steps in this book and surround yourself with others that support and encourage you to be the best you can be, you will find that your success is just around the corner.

If the advice and conversation within this book resonates with you, I would love to work with you. I work with clients on a personal basis and also in group mentoring programmes and trainings. Many of these can be done via the internet and I may be coming to a city near you in the not too distant future!

As you have read in this book, many clients come to me when they are feeling like 'something is missing'. This sometimes shows in miscommunication in relationships, not earning enough, not feeling good about yourself, not standing up for yourself or what you believe in, not succeeding in a career or new business, wanting more rapid career or business progress and YOU FEEL STUCK! Wherever you are, I would like to assist. Some clients prefer to start with the Group Mentoring programme. Then after seeing how we work, they schedule individual mentoring. It is entirely up to you and what you may need. You may feel you have enough information from this book for now but may want some mentoring or support in the near future. Whatever it is for you, commit to taking the right steps today, to figure out your purpose and live in Authentic Success. It is your birth- right.

I invite you to choose an option below and see you soon ♥ Put the link of your choice below in your computer browser and take ACTION TODAY!

1. I would love to work with you on a **Personal Mentoring** basis - www.amandasteadman.com/mentoring

2. I would love to be part of the NEXT **Group Mentoring Programme** – www.connecttosuccessacademy.com/mentoring

3. I'm good for now but would love to stay in touch and download your **BONUS AUTHENTIC SUCCESS RESOURCES – INSTANT ACCESS** www.amandasteadman.com/bonuses

4. I would like to contact Amanda directly please - Amanda@amandasteadman.com

I am excited to be working with you and connecting you to your authentic success. REMEMBER to download the FREE RESOURCES TOOL KIT that accompanies the book too. For instant access to YOUR FREE RESOURCES GO TO: www.amandasteadman.com/bonuses

To your health, wealth and success

Amanda ♥

Contact Amanda

Take action today and join our Authentic Success Programmes

Contact Amanda at www.amandasteadman.com/contact

or join our FREE Members Group at:
www.facebook.com/ConnectToSuccess

Or www.connecttosuccessacademy.com/contact

Or call us on +44 208 133 0675 or +1 721 527 5975

To Your Health, Wealth and Success!

Amanda

Amanda Steadman
Connect to Success
Author | Speaker | Mentor

FREE BONUS RESOURCES TOOL KIT –
@www.amandasteadman.com/bonuses

To get INSTANT ACCESS your downloadable the tools that accompany this book please put www.amandasteadman.com/bonuses into your browser. The page you will go to will have a box where you put your name, email and the Amazon Purchase Code.

You will then get an email link in your email inbox, so click on this to start downloading using your new tools RIGHT AWAY!

You will find:

✓ Connect to Authentic Success Mind Program MP3

✓ PDF HEART Goal Sheets

✓ PDF Example of a Written Goal in the HEART System

✓ Examples of 2 vision boards

✓ Other useful and fun goodies!

About the Author

Amanda Steadman

From a BA in Business & Languages to a successful career in the corporate as well as her own thriving business, Amanda has been in the field of human development for over 15 years and continues inspiring people to pursue their personal and business dreams. She invested thousands of dollars learning the latest, most effective, ways to maximize human potential and create inner success for herself and her clients using her exclusive techniques. In the corporate arena she assisted individuals to be 'successful' in business and in their careers, increasing profits and incomes, usually within 90 days. In one role Amanda tripled her income in a matter of months, and when she launched her own consultancy it reached 6 figures within 18 months!

Amanda is a Mom, Serial Entrepreneur, Trainer and Author, who speaks 5 languages and is on a mission to connect others to their 'true success'. She is happily married with two young daughters, travels, spends lots of time on the beach (and her laptop) and gets to do what she loves every day by living life 'on purpose' and keeping it simple.

www.amandasteadman.com

She is thrilled to be revealing all her secrets showing how she went from her life challenges to a life she dreamed of, explained in her new book *'Connect to Authentic Success: 7 Steps to the Destiny You Deserve'*. Amanda shares with readers how she went from total financial disaster and emotional doom to true authentic success.

"Wherever you are, whatever you are facing I will hold you by the hand and show you step-by-step how you can experience joy, confidence and satisfaction – the true ingredients to an authentic successful life."

♥

CONNECT TO AUTHENTIC SUCCESS: 7 STEPS TO THE DESTINY YOU DESERVE

AMANDA STEADMAN

© 2013 Published by **Amanda Steadman**

All Rights Reserved. No part of this publication may be reproduced in any form or by any means, including scanning, photocopying, or otherwise without prior written permission of the copyright holder.

First Printing, 2013

Printed Internationally.

www.amandasteadman.com
© Copyrighted Material

www.ingramcontent.com/pod-product-compliance
Lightning Source LLC
LaVergne TN
LVHW051603070426
835507LV00021B/2749